SPARKS that LEAP

For Roge and Paul,
Thank you so much
for your inspiration
and help. You are
true "soul mates."
Matt.

Edited by
Matt Morrison

For
James E. and Margaret A. Morrison
and
Parmenas and Lounette Cox
with love and gratitude

Typesetting and Book Design, Kevin S. Dunn.
Cover Design by Matt Morrison.
This book was written on a variety of word processing platforms, with final editing performed using Microsoft ® Word. Layout and design were performed on a desktop publishing system consisting of Apple Macintosh computers using Quark® X•Press.
Text and display type are Adobe Hiroshige.
Photographs and line art were input using an Abaton Scan 300/GS.
Final output was on a Apple Laserwriter IIntx.and Afga TabScript 300.
Printed in the United States of America

ISBN 0-89112-225-7
Library of Congress Card Number 91-73112

CONTENTS

Foreword

By its very definition, **a Christian university is a** different place—different from most institutions of higher education. The "differentness" does not come, however, by merely declaring it. Nor is it easily achieved. In fact, it is rather elusive.

The most distinctive element in our difference is our rare opportunity to present life as an integrated whole. The spiritual dimension, often ignored by practitioners of higher learning, is at the center of our instruction. Loving God and loving man are indeed the two most important tasks for all of us. No education is complete, or even liberal in the traditional sense, without a deep sense and appreciation of the spiritual elements which permeate our existence.

Our curriculum is ever in need of wholistic treatment, as well. We divide into colleges and departments and even sub-specialties within a discipline. All too often we present at worst an isolated view of learning and at best a piece-meal approach to its integration. It is no wonder that our students at times fail to see the connectedness of all these elements of what we call a "higher" education. In truth, its sum is always greater than the total of its individual parts. When we hold this awareness before our students, we are truly educating.

In our Christian environment, we also have the privilege of addressing the moral and ethical dimensions of life. Ours is not a value-free environment, and may it never be. We are convinced of that fact, but we must strive continually to set it into practice in a more effective manner. Derek Bok, outgoing president of Harvard University, told his Board of Overseers in 1988:

> Despite the importance of moral development to the individual student and the society, one cannot say that higher education has demonstrated a deep concern for the problem . . . . Universities will never do much to encourage a genuine concern for ethical issues or to help their students to acquire a strong and carefully considered set of moral values unless presidents and deans take the lead. . . .
>
> An equal responsibility rests with the faculty. . . . More than any other group, they set the tone of the institution, and establish what is important, what is legitimate, what truly merits the time and attention of the students. Unless professors recognize the importance of moral education, unless they personally participate by treating ethical issues in their classes, counseling students, helping to define and administer rules of behavior on campus, any

effort along these lines will lack credibility and force. Indeed, without such involvement, scholarly traditions of value-free inquiry may foster a sense among students and administrators that ethical questions are private matters to be kept out of serious conversation. . . .

One can appreciate the difficulty of the task and understand if progress is slow and halting. What is harder to forgive is a refusal to recognize the problem or to acknowledge a responsibility to work at it conscientiously. (*The Chronicle of Higher Education*, 27 April 1988: B4)

While we readily embrace Bok's admonition, we must also remind ourselves that the task and the progress is slow and halting. In an environment of a Christian university, we must ever call each other back to the essential rightness and necessity of the task of teaching morals and ethics and values to our students, remembering that our lives speak louder than our words.

The series of essays that is before you in this volume was conceptionalized and composed by people who embrace the wholistic view of learning that is the unique character of Christian education. All of us at the university and all who read these pages owe them a debt of gratitude for causing us to focus once again on the stirring challenges of teaching and learning in such an environment as ours at Abilene Christian University. Our mission of "educating students for Christian service and leadership throughout the world" is well served when we give continual attention to these forces that are part of our distinctive calling and heritage.

What a great privilege to be a part of a company of Christian scholars who see the value of developing the spiritual and moral aspects of our students, along with the intellectual and cultural dimensions! May we ever bind these elements together in what can truly be called a Christian education.

Royce Money, Ph.D.
President
Abilene Christian University
June 1991

Editor's Preface

A bright student asked me to recommend her to another school, a small private college in North Carolina. There, according to her friend, the students sit up nights and discuss ideas. "Here," she said, "to be honest—it's boring!" The ultimate insult. Also unfair. She was yet a freshman and had not given us a fair shot. If nothing exciting happens in the learning process, the student must share the blame.

But still, the challenge was hurled at our feet.

The need, as reflected in this incident, along with statements by Paul and Plato, led to the genesis of this book of essays.

Paul declares Christ the One "In whom are hid all the treasures of wisdom and knowledge" (Colossians 2:3). The articulate Christian teacher muses on things that are irresistibly interesting and charming—holding up in admiration a pearl or gem drawn from the vast treasurehouse of Jesus Christ—and in a rush of excitement feels *compelled* to share in the joy of discovery.

And then, there is the *student's* responsibility. Plato writes of long study and discussion of the truths of philosophy, when "a spark may suddenly leap, as it were, from mind to mind, and the light of understanding so kindled will then feed itself." I hope that more than a few sparks will leap and that more than a few will land.

The teacher who points out *everything* is a bore. She must, rather, inspire her students to reach. In my essay I have deliberately left some obvious gaps in supporting material. For one, there are no examples given of Christ's balance/rhythm in his dialogs (under II, *Play to the Ear*). Perhaps *you* can develop papers on this theme. In your study of the gospels, do you see any dominant conversational characteristics of Jesus? What texts? What words would you use to describe these features? What about His use of repetition, timing, surprise, restraint, and word play? How might a knowledge of New Testament Greek help you in this study?

The essays are arranged to reflect some of the ways Christ helps us in the search for the treasures of wisdom and knowledge, in relation

- to God (Allen, Morris),
- to ourselves (Morrison, Willerton),
- to others (Nichols, Mankin, McCormick),
- to our world (Keedy, Pfeifer),
- to our work (Lewis & Mitchell, Reinsch), and
- to our bodies (Hill).

Sincere thanks is tendered to each contributor. With the exception of William J. Mitchell (an MPA student at

Texas A & M), Marilyn Montgomery McCormick (a '75 alumnus and one of Marianna Rasco's fine products), and Hugh F. Keedy (an elder at the Otter Creek church of Christ and, for thirty-eight years, a Vanderbilt professor), each writer is a member of the ACU family.

I am especially grateful for Dwain Hart's support and confidence, and the wholehearted backing of President Royce L. Money and the members of this volume's advisory committee: Raye Lakey, James R. Nichols, Jeri Pfeifer, amd Lamar Reinsch. Thanks also to Paul Lakey for writing the excellent discussion questions.

The list of contributors in no way implies that these are the best writers of the various departments. A random selection from the entire pool of faculty would, no doubt, yield the same high quality. I hope that other faculty members—and students—will choose to contribute to subsequent volumes.

Kevin Dunn, as Macintosh guru, designer and formatter, continues to be invaluable. For the book's title logo, I got help from my oldest brother, Lewis. He scoured the ridges and patch orchards of Morgan County, West Virginia, for the perfect tool. The design was executed on a scrap of wallpaper with Maverick apple sticks, sharpened with an Old Timer penknife, by Schrade, 330T blade.

Matt Morrison
June 1991

1

Apprentice Under Heaven

On February 9, 1945, twenty-six-year-old Captain Solzhenitsyn, commander of a small artillery battalion, received a telephone call summoning him to his brigade headquarters. For months the Russian army had been driving the Germans back. In January they had mounted a great offensive to drive the enemy back through Poland all the way to Berlin. A brash and haughty commander, Solzhenitsyn had fought bravely and passionately in this offensive and had been decorated for his efforts.

When he entered headquarters, Brigidier-General Travkin ordered him to hand over his revolver, then said solemnly: "All right, you must go now."

Two officers from SMERSH, the Soviet counter-espionage service, immediately stepped forward and shouted, "You're under arrest!" They proceeded to rip the epaulettes from his shoulders, jerk his belt off, snatch the map-case from his hands, and turned to march him from the room.

Thus began Alexander Solzhenitsyn's harrowing and ultimately miraculous eight-year journey through what he later termed the Gulag Archipeligo, the island-like network of prisons and labor camps established by Stalin to crush dissent and further the Marxist transformation of Russian society.

Under Article 58 of the criminal code, Solzhenitsyn was convicted of "anti-Soviet agitation" and of founding a subversive organization. In reality, he had made the mistake, through a naive and idealistic commitment to Marxism, of criticizing Stalin. A few weeks later, with no hearing and no trial, he was sentenced to eight years in "corrective labour camps."

In the months that followed, Solzhenitsyn passed through several transit prisons. At each stage of his journey the ferocity of prison life stunned him. But at the same time he quickly grew wise in the ways of the camps. He learned, for example, that "persons with soft, accommodating expressions quickly died out on the islands." He also heard an inmate's solemn warning: "Above all, avoid 'general duties' like the plague. Avoid them from the very outset. If you land up on general duties on your first day, you're lost, lost forever!"

"General duties," Solzhenitsyn soon discovered, referred to the arduous labor assigned to eighty or ninety percent of the inmates in each camp. These jobs—like bricklaying, construction, digging clay, or smelting ore— were so demanding, and the work quotas set were so high, and the food so inadequate, that sooner or later most prisoners died from exhaustion and malnutrition. Solzhenitsyn determined to win one of the privileged jobs.

As the inmates were being called one by one to the director's office for their assignments, he put on his officer's uniform, complete with patent leather riding boots, hoping he would be singled out as a leader. His ploy worked, and he became a shift foreman in the clay pits. But his privileged status lasted only a few days. He was unable to drive his crew hard enough to meet the impossible quotas, and quickly found himself reassigned to general duties. The killing work quickly took its toll on him. The brigade continued to fall short of its quotas, and the men were put on punishment rations. Each received less than a pound of bread a day, three ladles of nearly inedible nettle broth and one of thin gruel. To compound the problems, rain fell day after day. The clay pit became a quagmire. Night after night the men slept in sopping-wet clothing in the cold and drafty barracks. Solzhenitsyn described a ringing in his head and felt himself on the brink of collapse. He had served only three weeks of his eight-year sentence.

But just when he felt his life slipping away, a reprieve came unexpectedly. He was transferred to Kaluga Gate, a labor camp on the outskirts of Moscow. In the months that followed, Solzhenitsyn began to gather strength. He learned the ways of the camps, the techniques of survival. And inside himself, hardly noticeable at first, he began gathering a different kind of strength, a moral and spiritual strength.

The people he met in the camps played an important role in his spiritual growth. In his first camp, for example, there was Boris Gammerov, a young Moscow intellectual. Gammerov spoke passionately of his belief in God and of his disdain for Stalin's Russia, and Solzhenitsyn was struck deeply not only by the man's Christian faith but also by his detached and defiant acceptance of his sentence. Solzhenitsyn himself had been raised in the bosom of the Russian Orthodox Church, but as a teenager had abandoned his faith and embraced Marxism with all the idealistic vigor of youth. And now, though for some unexplainable reason Stalin's agents had dealt him this crushing blow, he still could not doubt the ultimate righteousness and justice of the Marxist cause.

But over and over he met prisoners like Gammerov. He listened to men who had endured astounding hardship and yet retained a fanatical devotion to justice. He heard passionate denunciations of Soviet Marxism. He heard claims that it was a defunct political philosophy. Solzhenitsyn continued to defend his cause, but cracks began appearing in the bedrock of his convictions.

Those cracks deepened over the next three years. Through extraordinary good fortune, Solzhenitsyn found himself in a *sharashka*—a special prison institute where engineers, mathematicians, and other well-trained prisoners were gathered for scientific research. The living conditions were far better than the hard labor camps, and that probably saved his life.

There he met two men who left a deep mark on his thinking: Dimitri Panin and Lev Kopelev. Both were camp veterans and had suffered intensely. But they stood poles apart in their views. Kopelev remained a committed Marxist, believing that Stalin's purges were a gross error and that an all-wise Party soon would correct Stalin's errors. Panin, in contrast, was a dedicated Christian; he scorned Marxism and viewed the Bolsheviks as satanic instruments. Russia could be delivered from this evil, he believed, only by divine intervention.

Solzhenitsyn found himself steadily moving away from Kopelev's position and toward Panin's. But it was a great struggle. For awhile he found skepticism a convenient refuge, proclaiming, "I don't believe in anything, I don't know anything, leave me alone." But slowly he moved beyond skepticism. "I began gradually to return to my old, original childhood concepts," he later remembered. "I began to move ever so slowly towards a position . . . of supporting the primacy of the spiritual over the material." Still, he was not yet ready to tackle the question of religious belief.

In June 1950 Solzhenitsyn was transferred from the relatively humane *sharashka* to Ekibastuz, a huge hard labor camp on the frigid and wide-swept steppes of Soviet Central Asia. One of the extraordinary features of Solzhenitsyn's life in the camps thus far was his dedication to writing. And now, even in the desperate environs of Ekibastuz, he continued his work. "Sometimes in a sullen work party with machine-gunners barking around me," he later wrote, "lines and images crowded in so urgently that I felt myself borne through the air, overleaping the column in my hurry to reach the work compound and find a corner to write. At such moments I was both free and happy."

But writing nearly proved his undoing on several occasions. Once, for example, he was caught with a poem fragment and taken in for questioning. On the way, he crumpled the paper into a ball and dropped it on the ground. He then spent an anxious day and a sleepless night waiting for a chance to retrieve his poem, and even prayed for God's help. At five the next morning he went out into a howling wind and, after an hour of searching, finally found it. He thanked God fervently, and later wrote: "When things are bad, we are not ashamed of our God. We are ashamed of him only when things go well."

As the body of his poetry grew, it placed ever greater demands upon his powers of memory. So he devised an ingenuous system to insure that, in his regular reviews, he did not drop out lines. He saw that the Catholic Lithuanians in the camp made rosaries for themselves by soaking bread, forming beads with it, staining them black, white, and red, then stringing them on strands of thread. He asked the Lithuanians to make him one, but instead of the normal twenty, thirty, or forty beads, to use one hundred—with every tenth bead distinguishable by touch. They were amazed at what they took to be his religious zeal, and gladly assisted him.

With this makeshift "rosary" in hand, he would silently recite his poetry, moving a bead for each ten lines. "I fingered and counted my beads inside my wide mittens, at roll-call, on the march to and from work, at all times of waiting. I could do it standing up, and the freezing cold was no hindrance . . . . The warders found it on several occasions, but supposed that it was for praying and let me keep it." With this device Solzhenitsyn performed the astonishing feat of composing and memorizing 12,000 lines of poetry by the end of his sentence.

Solzhenitsyn's second year in Ekibastuz—and the seventh of his sentence—was a time of crisis and awakening. Early in 1952 he discovered a swelling in his abdomen and over the next few weeks it grew to the size of a lemon. The pain intensified and he was admitted to the camp hospital. The two doctors who examined him diagnosed cancer and scheduled him for immediate surgery. In a half-hour operation performed with only a local anaesthetic, a surgeon removed the tumor.

In the days that followed, something happened that would change his life forever. As he lay in the darkened recovery room one evening, Solzhenitsyn received a visit from a prison inmate and doctor named Boris Kornfeld. In the chapter in *The Gulag Archipeligo*, where Solzhenitsyn describes this visit and its impact on him, may be found the most eloquent and moving words he has ever written.

Kornfeld sat beside his bed and began talking. Solzhenitsyn was hot and feverish but able to listen clearly. This gentle and well-mannered doctor, whom Solzhenitsyn knew only slightly, began to tell the long story of his own conversion from Judaism to Christianity. He spoke with fervor and passion. He spoke, Solzhenitsyn remembered, with a "mystical knowledge in his voice." Hours passed. In his final words, Kornfeld spoke of transgression and suffering, and of how suffering more than anything else develops one's soul.

It was late, and the doctor slipped noiselessly into the dark corridor and then into one of the nearby wards to sleep. Solzhenitsyn slept. Everyone slept. But running and trampling noises awoke him early the next morning. Kornfeld's skull had been crushed with a plasterer's mallet, and orderlies were rushing him to the operating room. There he died without regaining consciousness.

Solzhenitsyn wrote that Kornfeld's final words "lay upon me as an inheritance." In the days that followed he lay there on his sick bed and with astonishment reflected back on his life. As was his long custom, he gathered his thoughts with poetry.

> When was it that I completely
> Scattered the good seeds, one and all?
> For after all I spent my boyhood
> In the bright singing of Thy temples.
>
> Bookish subtleties sparkled brightly,
> Piercing my arrogant brain,
> The secrets of the world were . . . in my grasp,
> Life's destiny . . . as pliable as wax.
>
> Blood seethed — and every swirl
> Gleamed iridescently before me,
> Without a rumble the building of my faith
> Quietly crumbled within my heart.
>
> But passing here between being and
> nothingness,

Stumbling and clutching at the edge,
I look behind me with grateful tremor
Upon the life that I have lived.

Not with good judgment nor with desire
Are its twists and turns illumined.
But with the even glow of the Higher Meaning
Which became apparent to me only later on.

And now with measuring cup returned to me,
Scooping up the living water,
God of the universe! I believe again!
Though I renounced You, You were with me!

Prison, he discovered, had restored his soul. Through the terrible buffeting of seven years in the camps, through times when his life hung as if by a thread, he discovered the most paradoxical of truths: "Your soul, which formerly was dry, is ripened by suffering."

Through this ripening, he learned the source of evil and of good. "In the intoxication of youthful successes," he confessed, "I had felt myself to be infallible, and I was therefore cruel . . . . In my most evil moments I was convinced that I was doing good, and I was well supplied with systematic arguments." But prison brought a moral awakening. "It was on rotting prison straw that I felt the first stirrings of good in myself. Gradually it became clear to me that the line separating good from evil runs not between states, not between classes, and not between political parties—it runs through the heart of each and every one of us, and through all human hearts. This line is not stationary. It shifts and moves with the passing of the years. Even in hearts enveloped in evil, it maintains a small bridgehead of good. And even the most virtuous heart harbors an unuprooted corner of evil."

With these words, we approach the heart of Solzhenitsyn's spiritual vision. In years to come he would flesh out that vision in stories, autobiographical novels, essays, and, much later, in his famous speeches. Through it all would run basic themes: the struggle for moral selfhood, the passion for truth and goodness, the predominance of the spiritual over the material, the necessity of suffering. But it all began here, in the camps, where spiritual fires seared and, in the end, refined his soul. For ever after he would look back with gratitude on his years in prison. "I nourished my soul there, and I say without hesitation: "Bless you, prison, for having been in my life."

Solzhenitsyn's eight years in the Gulag ended in February 1953. But he was still not quite a free man. From Ekibastuz armed guards escorted him and other released prisoners to the tiny village of Kok Terek near the China border. There for three years Solzhenitsyn lived as an exile. He found employment as a high school physics teacher, and excelled in his work. But writing remained his passion. With absolute secrecy and uncommon self-discipline, he devoted every spare hour to it. He first put down on paper the great volume of poetry he had written and memorized in the camps. Then he wrote two verse plays, both attempting to synthesize what he had learned about Russian history and society in the camps.

While in exile Solzhenitsyn faced cancer a second time. He was forced to spend six weeks receiving radiation treatment in the distant city of Tashkent. Doctors pronounced that his chances for recovery were one in three. Fighting despair, he returned to Kok Terek and his writing. Recovery was swift, and Solzhenitsyn later wrote that the cure was "a divine miracle; I could see no other explanation. Since then, all the life given back to me has not been mine in the full sense: it is built around a purpose." This sense of divine mission remained with him, helping to sustain his enormous capacity for work and, later, his heroic struggle against the Soviet government.

When his exile was lifted in 1956, Solzhenitsyn was reunited with his wife and settled in the modest city of Ryazan not far from Moscow. Again, he taught high school physics and astronomy, and demonstrated a marvelous gift in the classroom. But, though no one knew it but his wife, his primary vocation was writing. Over the next six years he worked on three autobiographical novels: *The First Circle*, about his years in the *sharashka*; *One Day in the Life of Ivan Denisovitch*, reflecting his experiences in Ekibastuz; and *Cancer Ward*, growing out of his stay in the Tashkent hospital.

All through these years, Solzhenitsyn took remembrance of his life in the camps and in exile as a sacred duty. Each year on the anniversary of his arrest, he undertook a symbolic return to prison. For his morning meal, he cut himself 23 ounces of bread and dissolved two sugar cubes in hot water. Then at noon he ate a bowl of broth and a ladle of groats and in the evening the rest of the bread and more groats. Describing the effects, he wrote: "How quickly I get back to my old form. By the end of the day, I am already picking up crumbs to put in my mouth and licking the bowl. The old sensations start up vividly."

In addition to this yearly ritual, Solzhenitsyn also treasured mementos from the camps—his old jacket and number patches, the aluminum spoon he had fashioned for himself, his battered suitcase with its bayonet hole. He treasured them almost like "holy relics," for they were the indelible reminders of the pilgrimage which had harrowed and then hallowed his soul.

In May of 1959 Solzhenitsyn seized upon another "relic" from the camps—an idea for a story. He had gotten the idea while laying bricks in Ekibastuz. He began writing and in just under six weeks completed a short novel. It was later entitled *One Day in the Life of Ivan Denisovitch*. The story set down in a kind of rich and concentrated shorthand much of Solzhenitsyn's experience in the camps. In the central character, Ivan Denisovitch, Solzhenitsyn embodied one of his most important themes: the immense capacity of human beings to absorb pain and injustice and yet emerge with at least a vestige of their humanity intact.

But in the story it is Alyosha the Baptist, not Ivan, who represents Solzhenitsyn's Christian ideal. In a climactic scene in the story, Alyosha overhears Ivan's whispered prayer, and says: "There you are, Ivan Denisovitch, your soul is begging to pray. Why don't you give it its freedom?" Ivan sighs and says: "Prayers are like those appeals of ours. Either they don't get through or they're returned with 'rejected' scrawled across 'em."

But Alyosha insists that Ivan does not pray hard enough and that when he does pray, he focuses too much on material things. Christ commanded only that one pray for his daily bread, Alyosha insisted; beyond that, "We must pray about things of the spirit—that the Lord Jesus should remove the scum of anger from our hearts." Ivan responds that, when he prays, it will be for tangible things—like release from his unjust prison sentence.

Alyosha counters with dismay in his voice: "What do you want your freedom for? What faith you have left will be choked in thorns. Rejoice that you are in prison. Here you can think of your soul." Ivan remains confused, but thinks: "Alyosha was speaking the truth. His voice and his eyes left no doubt that he was happy in prison."

The story of Ivan and Alyosha was published in the Soviet Union in late 1962 (and to this day remains the only one of Solzhenitsyn's books published there). The first 100,000 copies sold out nearly overnight. The 850,000 copies printed a few weeks later also sold out immediately. An English translation appeared just weeks later.

Solzhenitsyn's fame throughout the world was instant and enormous. Critics compared him to Tolstoy and Dostoyevsky. Letters poured in by the thousands.

From 1962 until his expulsion from the country in 1974, Solzhenitsyn waged a long and courageous struggle against the Soviet authorities. Quickly realizing their mistake in publishing the story, the government gradually mounted a campaign to silence him. But Solzhenitsyn would not be silenced. He wrote bold public appeals, including a letter of 1970 entitled "Live Not by Lies."

In the midst of Soviet attempts to silence and discredit him, the Swedish Academy awarded Solzhenitsyn the Nobel Prize for Literature in 1970, but he was not allowed to leave Russia and accept it in person. The vilification campaign against him escalated. He received telephone calls threatening murder, poisoning of his food, and even harm to his children. Finally in February 1974, he was arrested and deported to the West. Only his worldwide fame had saved his life.

Though Solzhenitsyn eventually found a home in Vermont, where he still lives, his true home remains the labor camps of Stalin's Russia. He found his soul there. He nourished his faith there. He grew strong there. There he watched Marx die and Jesus rise from the grave. There he discovered the source of Truth, Goodness, and Beauty, and so learned to loathe lies. There, as he embraced the eternal, he discovered the beauty of the temporal. There, in the camps, he passed through death and so learned to hear the voice of God. And there too Solzhenitsyn the Christian writer was born.

In his Nobel Lecture of 1970, Solzhenitsyn contrasts two kinds of writers or artists. One kind imagines himself autonomous, "the creator of an independent spiritual world." This writer is doomed to fail, for human beings can never create a stable system alone.

The other kind of writer "acknowledges a higher power above him and joyfully works as a common apprentice under heaven." He works in "a world about whose foundations he has no doubt." As a result, his task is "to sense more keenly than others the harmony of the world, the beauty and the outrage of what man has done to it, and poignantly to let people know." The artist, in short, is called to tell the truth about the dual nature of humankind, about Creation and Fall. In this, he becomes God's apprentice.

Both in his literature and his public pronouncements, Solzhenitsyn attempts to tell this truth. Even in America. Far from rejoicing in the celebrated freedoms of American democracy, Solzhenitsyn decries the pride and spiritual flabbiness it produces. He decries America's ever increasing pursuit of material affluence, believing it leads to spiritual and even physical destruction. He believes, instead, in the hard way. He believes that true freedom lies only in self-limitation; that we grow strong in the prisons and the dark pits of this world. For there we have time to think about our souls. There we grow spiritually ripe. There, above all, we find the dividing line between evil and good.

C. Leonard Allen, Ph.D.
Associate Professor of Bible
Abilene Christian University

Questions

1. Describe Solzhenitsyn's journey/struggle that led him to God and faith.

2. What could you use besides beads to aid your memorization of God's word?

3. Examine Solzhenitsyn's poem (pp. 7-8). What does the poem tell you about the road to faith? Compare Romans 7:24-8:1 to the message of the poem.

4. Solzhenitsyn claims that Americans have become spiritually flabby with their "material affluence." How do you respond to his declarations?

5. Solzhenitsyn believes that we "grow strong in the prisons and the dark pits of this world." Provide an example of our prisons and dark pits.

6. How can you apply the Solzhenitsyn story to your life?

2

Are We Free?

"I see nobody on the road," said Alice.
"I only wish I had such eyes," The King remarked in a fretful
tone. "To be able to see Nobody! And at that distance, too!
Why, it's as much as I can do to see real people, by this
light!"
        Alice's Adventures in Wonderland
        by Lewis Carroll

'**H**ow can you believe in God?" "If God is good, how do you explain the existence of evil and suffering in this creation?" "How do you justify belief in free-will and thus moral responsibility?" These are questions which have been posed to me by fellow students or scientists at one time or another in my career. They are questions with which every thinking Christian will have to deal. I had to grapple with the problems personally to solidify and clarify my beliefs. But in my dealings with others, I found I could be taken seriously only by having considered these problems in depth. I would lose credibility by ignoring the problems and my communications with these friends on religious topics would break down. I must avoid the attitude of Samuel Johnson, who said, "Sir, we know our will is free, and there's an end on't."

Through much reading, study, and conversation, I have arrived at positions on these questions which, while not logically unassailable, are satisfactory for me. In this essay, I will deal only with the problem of free-will/determinism. As of now there is no perfect solution, and I believe that there never will be. This does not mean that we should ignore the question because it is of mere academic importance. There are people who unconsciously or consciously are determinists—many in order to avoid moral responsibility. My essay will be heuristic or suggestive and not a technical treatise. I will not rehash the standard arguments, but will deal only with the impact of discoveries in modern science and logic of paradox.

The problems are illustrated in the following conversation between two students:

Joe: Bob, let's go out tonight and party!

Bob: I can't, Joe. I have to study for a physics exam tomorrow.

Joe: What? Haven't you learned from physics that everything is determined. It doesn't matter how much you study the course, your life is set in stone. Everything has a cause and the chain of cause-effect is inexorable in the future. You can't do anything about it. If you fail, you fail; if you pass, you pass!

Bob: Joe, I feel like I am responsible. I feel like I have free-will and that study can indeed influence the grade I make on the exam.

Joe: You feel responsible? That feeling is determined; you can't help feeling that. Events are either produced by cause and effect, in which case the events are determined; or events occur randomly without cause, as in quantum theory. Either way, you cannot legitimately believe you have personal responsibility!

Bob: Physics puts forth two contradictory ideas. That leads me to believe that maybe physics doesn't deal with everything. I will continue to believe that I am responsible for myself and study for the exam.

Joe: Well, Bob, have fun! It is determined that I party tonight.

The paradox is at least as old as recorded history. The Greek Democritus (ca. 400 B.C.) postulated a materialistic universe of atoms, each of which had a trajectory determined for all time. St. Augustine introduced determinism in the form of predestination into Christianity. With the success of Newtonian physics, determinism became a much more intellectually acceptable system. Some of the more well-known determinists are philosophers Baruch Spinoza, Arthur Schopenhauer, and Friedrich Nietzsche; attorney Clarence Darrow; physicist Albert Einstein; and psychologist B. F. Skinner.

How did this respectability come about? In 1686, Sir Isaac Newton published *The Mathematical Principles of Natural Philosophy*, which is without question the most influential scientific publication in the history of man. Mathematically, Newton's physics says that given the position and velocity of a particle at any given time, its future can be determined. So successful were Newton's ideas that during the eighteenth century many people tried, unsuccessfully, to find the "laws" of a "social physics" to explain the behavior of human beings. Adam Smith's *The Wealth of Nations* was such an attempt. The universe was thought to operate like a giant clockwork mechanism; God wound it up initially and there was no further need for His involvement.

The eighteenth-century mathematician and astronomer Pierre Simon Laplace took the extreme determinist position. Given a large enough calculator and the position and velocity of all particles in the world, Laplace believed that he could determine the future state of the universe at any given time.

How can we argue with this success of science? Science has put men on the moon, produced three-inch television and extremely high-speed computers, discovered medicines and procedures which extend our lives tremendously, and developed weapons which can remove life from the face of the earth. Deterministic science must describe reality, it is too successful not to! How can I help but believe in determinism?

Physics and Indeterminism

As a first response, I would say that present-day science is not a monolith of determinism. In fact, possibly the most successful scientific theory developed so far, the quantum theory, is an inherently indeterministic theory. The quantum theory is the theory of the atomic world and is responsible for the development of the laser, computers, superconductors, and other solid-state devices. According to the quantum theory, there are certain events which can never be predicted but rather occur completely at random. Let me emphasize that this is not a direct argument for free-will but rather an argument against determinism. If our acts are random, we can have no more moral responsibility than if the acts are determined. All science is not deterministic.

For the physicist, light is a very important, complex, and mysterious phenomena. The characteristics of light help fix the nature of the physical universe and our perceptions of it. Albert Einstein in 1905 created quite a stir among physicists when he stated that the nature of light depends on what we do to observe it. Sometimes it acts as a hard, concentrated (though very small) pellet (particle); sometimes it behaves as a water wave diffusely hitting the beach. We can understand light as a wave or we can understand it as a particle, but how can we understand it as both?

In order to explain this, the creative and radical physicist Niels Bohr (1913) put forth the so-called complementarity principle—waves and particles give complementary descriptions of light. Neither description by itself is sufficient. Bohr then took a highly speculative leap from physics to extend the principle to our lives.

Suppose a biologist takes a living plant and starts cutting until she reaches a molecular level. The life does not exist at that level. Life has been destroyed in order to find out something about life. This atomistic approach cannot give us a full explanation; the whole plant approach cannot give us satisfactory information about the genetics of the plant. Somehow, neither the holistic nor atomistic approach is satisfactory by itself; both are required for a complete description—they are complementary.

Maybe free-will and determinism are complementary aspects of our existence. If we view the human being from the point of view of physics, maybe the being is determined. If we look on the human as a moral being, free-will becomes important. Neither is satisfactory by itself; both are necessary for a complete description.

The key here is that we cannot conceive of the coexistence of waves and particles or of free-will and determinism. In gestalt psychology, there is a well know rabbit/duck diagram.

Looking at the diagram one way, you see a rabbit; while looking at it another way, you see a duck. You cannot see them both at the same time. Perhaps our inability to conceive of simultaneous free-will/determinism is analogous to the impossibility of perceiving the rabbit and the duck at the same time.

The Nature of Science

"It is wrong to think that the task of physics is to find out how nature is. Physics concerns what we can say about nature" [Niels Bohr]. This statement leads me to a second set of problems which I believe contribute to the free-will/determinism argument, and that is the nature of science. What is science? Is it a metaphysical description of reality or is it a "short-end" technique which allows us to make use of nature? Beliefs in these positions have waxed and waned since the beginnings of science, ca. 600 B.C.

Galileo was allowed, by his "friend" Pope Urban, to teach that the sun-centered universe produced an easier mathematical description than an earth-centered universe. He was forbidden to take the next step and say that the sun is at the center of the universe.

Science in the eighteenth and nineteenth centuries was believed to explain the real universe. This led to a worshipping of science in what is called "scientism." The only accepted explanations were those of science. If questions could not be answered scientifically, they were irrelevant. For example, "Is there a God?" and "Is that rose more beautiful than a mud clod?" are both irrelevant according to that view. Since physics was a determined system and since it described reality, everything must be determined and there is no free-will.

We can be thankful that the twentieth century has produced a much more sophisticated and less arrogant view of science. I will briefly present a representative position from the noted Austrian philosopher of science, Sir Karl Popper.

Science is not merely a catalogue of experience. We develop science in order to manage the catalogue and to try to understand the totality of our world experiences. Science compresses certain aspects of our human experience into a manageable form.

Karl Popper believes that science is like a net into which all of our experience are poured. The net allows some experiences to fall through while others are trapped. These trapped experiences form the substance or data for our science. There are three observations that I would like to make (from this grossly oversimplified picture):

1. Many, in fact most, experiences are not included in the science. Perhaps there are those experiences for which the will is free which are never captured by the net.
2. How the net is constructed can also be a

factor in what the net will capture. Perhaps the net traps events related by apparent cause and effect. Science likes cause and effect; in fact science has totally ignored the catastrophic attack on the cause-effect concept by the eighteenth century Scottish philosopher David Hume.

3. There is a personal (subjective) element in determining the structure of the net. There are certain decisions which must be made, where the determining factor can only be personal.

What I am trying to say is that science is great but it is not all encompassing. We should take science with great seriousness, but we should not assign it an absolute superiority over other forms of knowledge. We must not take a partial truth and make it total.

The Jewish philosopher Martin Buber has given an excellent example of the difference between the way a person is related to another person (I-Thou, human relations) and the way the person is related to an object (I-It, science). The I-It relationship is one of objective analysis and manipulative control of impersonal objects. I-Thou relationships are characterized by involvement of the whole self and concern for the other person as an end in himself. The I-Thou meeting can be entered into but it cannot be reduced to the realm of space, time, and causality — the world of "It."

The Problems of Logic

The first study of logic was undertaken by Aristotle around 350 B.C. However, it is not until the twelfth and thirteenth centuries, with the Catholic theologians Anselm and

22

Thomas Aquinas, that reason or logic becomes preeminent in Western thought. During the eighteenth century, this reliance on logic was boosted by the success of mathematical science, which is the supreme achievement of human reason.

During the nineteenth century a systematic, critical study of logic was begun. Bertrand Russell was especially concerned with paradoxical statements which apparently had no resolutions under logical analysis. Russell gives his 'Barber Paradox':

> A barber shaves all individuals who do not shave themselves. Who shaves the barber?

A logical contradiction arises regardless of whether he shaves himself or not. The oldest known such paradox originated around 600 B.C.:

> Epimenides, the Cretan, says, 'All Cretans are liars.'

If he is telling the truth he is lying; and if he is lying, he is telling the truth. You are probably familiar with the placard with the following statement on side one:

> The statement on the opposite side is true.

And flipping over, the statement on side two:

The statement on the opposite side is false.

Oh, what to believe!

Much of comedy is based on these kinds of paradoxes. Groucho Marx has a famous, funny line:

I wouldn't want to belong to any club that would have me as a member.

From Joseph Heller's *Catch-22* comes the ultimate statement of the paradoxes arising in modern society:

There was only one catch and that was Catch-22, which specified that a concern for one's own safety in the face of dangers that were real and immediate was the process of a rational mind. Orr was crazy and could be grounded. All he had to do was ask; and as soon as he did, he would no longer be crazy and would have to fly more missions. Orr would be crazy to fly more missions and sane if he didn't, but if he was sane he had to fly them. If he flew them he was crazy and didn't have to; but if he didn't want to he was sane and had to.

For those who take logic as absolute, these paradoxes are serious problems and they must be dealt with.

In 1931, Kurt Gödel, a Viennese mathematician settled the problem. He proved that a finite logical system can not be shown to be consistent (Gödel's Theorem). This means that in any logical system there can arise contradictory statements, neither of which can be shown to be false. So much for perfect logical knowledge.

Most of the problems which arise are called self-referential, that is, the statements refer to themselves in one way or another. It has been suggested that free-will/determinism is a paradox within science just for this reason. (I omit the technical philosophical argument.) Science, which is supposedly objective, viewing the subjective self creates a logical contradiction of self-reference which may be explained by Gödel's Theorem.

Whether or not this is actually the case, Gödel's Theorem does make us chary about making absolute statements concerning any logical system. Neither determinism nor free-will has been demonstrated to be true in the logic of modern science.

Conclusion

I do not want to throw out science and logic as methods of learning because they are the most successful tools we have. We must however learn that there are limits to their applicability, and we must be constantly aware that we are finite beings trying to comprehend with our science, logic, and language an infinite system of knowledge.

If we have no free will, it does not matter what we believe because we could not do otherwise. On the other hand, if we do have free will and choose the determinists' views in order to avoid moral responsibility, we can produce considerable damage, not only to ourselves but also to our society. I personally do not know the answer to the free-will/determinism enigma, yet I must live. Using scientific terminology, I use free will as an hypothesis to guide my life, while letting my mind wonder at this free-will/determinism dualism with which the best minds throughout history have grappled.

Maybe we *are* able to see the King's Nobody—or maybe we have created a free-will/determinism paradox which is a pseudo-problem. It's as much as we can do to handle real problems with the "light" of our science and logic.

Paul Morris, Ph.D.
Professor of Physics
Abilene Christian University

Questions

1.   What is the concept of free will?

2.   What is the concept of determinism?

3.   What is meant by "Neither determinism nor free will has been demonstrated to be true in the logic of modern science"?

4.   Dr. Morris asks, "Are we free?" How would you answer?

5.   Are science and faith incompatible? Defend your answer.

3

Lord, Teach Us to See

"In the beginning was the Word, and the Word was with God, and the Word was God. The same was in the beginning with God. All things were made by him; and without him was not any thing made that was made. In him was life; and the life was the light of men." (John 1:1-4)

"That was the true Light, which lighteth every man that cometh into the world." (John 1:9)

"In whom are hid all the treasures of wisdom and knowledge." (Colossians 2:3)

"Lift up your eyes, and look . . . ." (John 4:35)

Jesus Christ is the Light of all human enlightenment and the Source of all treasures of wisdom and knowledge. Man's feeble attempts at rhetoric, and indeed every sound and rhythm of nature, are faint and tinny resonances of the eternal Word. We must remember, as Rudolf Arnheim cautions, that the Word, *logos*, does not mean "word" in our sense, "but rather reason underlying the cosmos and creation of order" (Peterson 55). To Arnheim, vision is the primary medium of thought to access reason (18).

Oh, if only we could think as smart as we see, talk as smart as we think, and write as smart as we talk.

Jesus taught us how to see. Observe how fickle children change their games in marketplace play, how a spoiled son's return from a far country affects his older brother, and how a distraught housewife searches for a lost coin.

I believe that our openness to enlightenment—especially in reading and writing—might be prescribed in two irreducible cryptic imperatives: (1) read to the eye; (2) play to the ear.

Read to the Eye

A writer should use image-evoking language to enable the reader to *read to the eye.* Sir E. A. Wallis Budge, late Keeper of the Egyptian and Syrian Antiquities in the British Museum, pointed out that hieroglyphic characters were written in columns or in horizontal lines, which are sometimes to be read from left to right and sometimes from right to left. To discover the direction in which an inscription is to be read, "we must observe in which way the men, and birds, and animals face, and then read towards them." This example from Funeral Stele of Panehesi (XIXth dynasty), with phonetic values and English translation, demonstrates this clearly.

| qemam | unenet | en | ātu |
| creator | of {things which shall be, | [and] of | animals, |

Thus, by graphic analogy, the ancients remind us to read to the open face—the open eye (10-11, 216).

All learning begins with *seeing.*

The image is primary and can leapfrog over a stubborn blockade of words. The political cartoonist, for example, aims at a purposeful condensation of sometimes complex meanings into a single striking image. Robeson County, North Carolina, has a 35 percent Native American

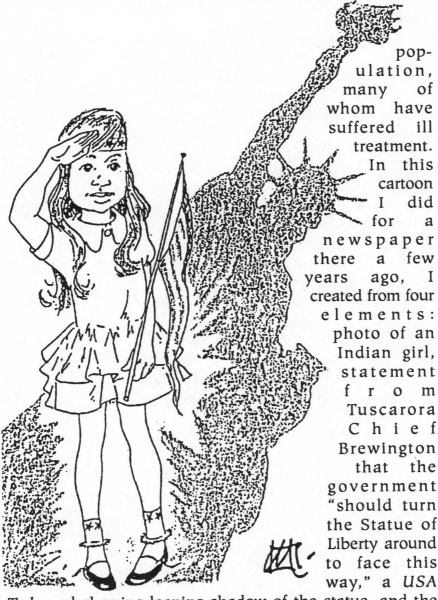

pop-ulation, many of whom have suffered ill treatment. In this cartoon I did for a newspaper there a few years ago, I created from four elements: photo of an Indian girl, statement from Tuscarora Chief Brewington that the government "should turn the Statue of Liberty around to face this way," a *USA Today* ad showing leaning shadow of the statue, and the collective memory of the community.

I discussed this cartoon with my advertising students. Later, on a test, they were asked:

29

In the Statue of Liberty cartoon, why is the girl saluting?

    a. as a visual foil to the torch arm
    b. to celebrate freedom
    c. to show that Native Americans' freedom pre-dated our own
    d. all of the above

Of course, the answer is d, "all of the above."

Cartoonists can abuse truth through graphic glibness. A comparison which makes the abstract real or the unfamiliar clearer gives us the satisfaction of pretended insight. Like children who "understand" our solar system when told it is like a basketball and nine marbles, we are easily fobbed off with an answer. The power of the cartoon is its weakness.

Visual literacy leads to *metaphor* literacy when reflective thought generates new connections. A poet observes an injured starling on his daughter's bedroom floor. The bird tries to escape through the open window. Finally it succeeds. The poet discovers a similarity to the girl's emerging independence: "She cleared the window sill of the world."

I've often wondered on the maturation of the young boy Jesus growing up in Nazareth, as we find described in Luke 2:52: "And Jesus increased in wisdom and stature, and in favour with God and man." His pristine curiosity, His edge of intensity to confirm revealed truth in the face of nature, is later verified in His apt use of metaphor.

Jesus closely observed common objects, animals, and human nature. In His teaching method, Jesus gave us entry into His *instructive* and *persuasive* mind. Indeed, our Lord's inventive method—fluency in the generation of fresh metaphor based on confidence in the validity of human experience and the essential nature of things—is emulated (not always by conscious design) by our celebrated literary giants.

F. Scott Fitzgerald wrote that he, Thomas Wolfe and Ernest Hemingway had a "family resemblance," since all three were attempting "to recapture the exact feel of a moment in time and space, exemplified by people rather than by things. . . an attempt at a mature memory of a deep experience" (Turnbull 224, 251). Wolfe's eye was unfailing:

> My Brother Ben's face, thought Eugene, is like a piece of slightly yellow ivory; his high white head is knotted fiercely by his old man's scowl; his mouth is like a knife, his smile the flicker of light across a blade. (Wolfe 137)

Wolfe recalls his first meeting with Mrs. Margaret Roberts, the high school teacher he idolized:

> He turned his face up to her as a prisoner who recovers light, as a man long pent in darkness who bathes himself in the great pool of dawn, as a blind man who feels upon his eyes the white core and essence of immutable brightness. (Wolfe 178)

What Fitzgerald calls "a mature memory" is nurtured through a perky, wide-eyed way of looking at things.

One Friday afternoon several years ago our son bounded in the back door. "Dad! Come quick—there's something in the yard!" He ran ahead of me to point to a movement under the sod. With a shovel I unearthed a fat squirmy mole, plunked the furry little monster into a Mason jar, screwed the lid shut, and with a steak fork punched air holes in the lid. He planned to take it to school Monday morning for Show and Tell. But that night it died. Mason-jar shock. We carried it up a hill, dug a little hole, erected a twig cross and had a funeral.

I said, "Matt, say something."

His brown eyes wide, "What do I say, Dad?"

"Well, Son, you say what you can about the mole"— I gave it my best Walter Brennan—"he came from the ground and he's goin' back to the ground. He never did nobody no harm."

Matt was challenged by the task of rhetorical invention—finding what to say. He could use the topics of origin, destination, and purpose to jump-start his funeral oration. Invention, the first of the five canons of classical rhetoric, is action which generates the new. It is the substance of learning.

Aristotle said, "Learning things and wondering at things" are pleasant. Wondering, he said, "implies the desire of learning." So that, he added, "the object of wonder is an object of desire; while in learning one is brought into one's natural condition" (Book I, ch. 11, 1371a. 30-34).

Learning and wondering restore our natural condition.

Recently, an encyclopedia salesman called to set up a meeting.

"I sent that card in a year ago," I said. "I want to talk to your marketing people to propose your underwriting a children's television show, a Look it Up segment. Show kids learning by looking things up in the encyclopedia."

"Well, yah," he said, "but ah, on television you gotta do it like *Sesame Street*. Make it fun like that. You can't do it with an encyclopedia."

"I don't agree," I said. "Kids get real satisfaction and pleasure out of learning. Here in the Southwest we are fighting anti-intellectualism and peer pressure. From middle school on, no boy is seen carrying a book home. Reading is for nerds. Real guys play football and real girls lead cheers for the non-readers. And in university book stores they push cheese curls and Pepsis."

"Well, yeah," he conceded, "you do have the anti, er, whatever you call it."

Children seem beset by hostile aliens who would sully the real world of their imaginations. In the *Empire of the Sun* movie the boy reached back for his toy Zero. He gave up security with his parents for a world of imagination—always a risk. But through this choice he was able to survive the five years in a prison camp. Near the end of the movie the Doctor friend had to bring him back: "Try not to *think* so much!"

I have students sitting in my classes who defiantly tuned out at thirteen or fourteen, some earlier—dulled by learning. Now we must desperately fan the embers. In too many of our schools, language is for learning, grammar is deadly serious stuff, Shakespeare is for SAT points.

> Dull teaching will clip an angel's wings,
> Conquer all mysteries by rule and line,
> Empty the haunted air, and gnomed mine—
> (paraphrase of Keats, "Lamia,"
> II, 234-236)

I hold five spoons which I bought at 20 cents each at the 1985 Great Buffalo Gap Chili Cook-off and Flea Market. The chili was good; the rattlesnake meat was a bit gamy. When I got home I had a good time polishing these spoons and studying their markings. No two are alike in design. Here's one from the Blackstone Hotel. I like their balance, bounce and sound. But what's their significance? Maybe they're worth a *Sports*

Illustrated sentence: "Like a mismatched set of flea-market spoons, the Celtics' starting five—worn yet polished—turned in a sterling performance."

Fascination and observation come first.

To paraphrase painter Ben Shahn, intuition comes only after prolonged tuition (124). Significance is an afterthought. But it is a thought. There is no detail or commonplace without meaning.

*Pencil and Craypas drawing
Erin Dunlap, Taylor Elementary*

In my Cody Coyote Art Club at a local elementary school, I had the children drawing and painting twigs and leaves: "Now, you've got to look closely at all the rich colors and tiny veins on the leaves and the little bumps and nodules on the twigs." After about twenty minutes of working on his pencil drawing, Charlie, a first-grader, scroonched up his face, tilted his head and said, "This is really *hard!*" It was the supreme compliment. For concentration—*total engagement*—is an increasingly rare commodity in the classroom.

If all learning begins with seeing, the teacher should be constantly alert to bring each learning activity back to that basic skill. For a writer, vivid impression precedes clear expression. Whatever tends to present the thing spoken of, George Campbell said, "to the notice of our senses, especially of our eyes, greatly enlivens the expression" (291).

Play to the Ear

Reclaim the same unselfconscious love of language you once had as a child. Read aloud: tease out the linguistic melodies of the printed page, realize the literature—*play to the ear*.

Here is an excerpt of a lesson I gave to a second grade class:

> The Zuni Indians. Z-u-n-i. And it's pronounced Zoon'ye. The Zoon'ye Indians of New Mexico say that—
>> When the coyote sees the blackbird dancing,
>> he is beside himself with joy;
>> when he sees the ravens laugh,
>> he sticks his tail straight up
>> out of sheer sympathy.

photograph by John Paul Brownlow

Sometimes—sometimes—his voice is as idle as a cricket's chirp. You know what a cricket's chirp is? It's the chirp of a cricket.

Student: Also, a cricket can make a sound on its face.

Right. How do they do that?

Student: They put their legs together and they pull them back and forward.

And it makes a sound and it's nice and easy like the cricket's chirp. Sometimes it fills the valley like a mist fills the valley—it's going to have a lot of echo. Let's do it. Ow-w-w-w-w. Did you hear it? Did you hear it fill the valley like a mist?

A child's language is creative, artistic, instructive and rhetorical. As Naremore and Hopper remind us, young children display "a vivacity in communicating and learning that can serve as a model for everyone" (1).

It was the Patriarch Job who asked, "Doth not the ear try words? And the mouth taste his meat?" (Job 12:11)

Here are two bits of writing. The layout of each helps the reader recreate the balance and rhythm of the spoken language. The first is a note from a second-grade boy—reflecting an unselfconscious love of language. The second is a Macy's newspaper ad—demonstrating a reclaimed love of language.

Ungaro Uomo

The Man
Was a Ham
But He Was a Can:
And He Was
a cat:
And a:

fat: And Mat:

Clothes that go with the flow.

And move with the body.

Subtly draped to create a powerful shape.

Above Left This note from a second-grader reveals an unselfconscious love of language.
Above A Macy's ad mirrors the same fascination.

Carl A. Lefevre cautions that language should be treated as speech, with constant cross-references among speech, writing and reading. The child's invention of his language "begins with large melodic and rhythmic patterns" and by the time she enters school can read aloud and can discover "how the graphic counterparts of the language system provide useful clues to the melodies of the printed page" (35,44).

All language has rhythm.

As thought takes shape in the speaker's mind, it takes a shape. Rhythm is organically related to thought. This is true in prose; it is certainly true in music—words set to music.

By inducing in us a pattern of expectancy and playing against that the surprise of variation, performers can make us realize both sense and emotion more intensely. Expectancy and variation keep the listener alert and participating in the communicative process.

Robert Johnson was a Mississippi country blues singer and guitarist, born about 1910. He was murdered, likely by a jealous lover, in 1938. He put down twenty-nine of his songs for the old Vocalion label in 1936 and 1937.

Griel Marcus in *Mystery Train* said Johnson was working out a whole new aesthetic that rock 'n' roll eventually completed: a loud, piercing music driven by massive rhythms and a beat so strong that involvement was effortless and automatic (30).

> She's a kind-hearted woman,
> She studies evil all the time.
>
> She's a kind-hearted woman,
> She studies evil all the time.
>
> You well's to kill me,

As to have it on your mind.

What evil does she study? We are told in the third couplet. Our insight is the satisfaction we derive from listening.

Notice the *antithesis* scheme, the juxtaposition of contrasting ideas in parallel structure. This is a common form in blues: repetition of the first couplet, followed by the surprise in the third. We see it in this Jimmy Rodgers song:

> I'd rather drink muddy water,
> And sleep in a hollow log.
>
> I'd rather drink muddy water,
> And sleep in a hollow log.
>
> Than to be in Atlanta,
> And treated like a dirty dog.

Our **talk** is balanced. We tend to balance phrases of more or less equal auditory weight. In his discussion of prose rhythm, Aristotle advised that the pattern of the diction "should be rhythmical, but not metrical, or we should have, not prose, but verse." The rhythm must not be too precise and must be natural to the character (Cooper 199-200). Terry Malloy, in Budd Schulberg's screenplay of *On the Waterfront*, says to his brother:

> It was **you**, Charley. You was my **bro**ther.
> You should of looked **out** for me. Instead of
> making me take them **dives** for the **short**-end
> money.

If you recall Marlon Brando's performance, the actor laid stress on **you**, **bro**ther and **out** in the first three short sentences—in harmony with the emotional realism of the scene.

In the Cody Coyote lesson, notice how I repeat to accommodate my listeners: "Sometimes—sometimes—his voice is as idle as a cricket's chirp. You know what a cricket's chirp is? It's the chirp of a cricket."

When we encounter effective expression today, we are likely to recognize in it not only the pure rhetoric of Jesus, but also the tracings and echoes of nature.

> We are led to believe a Lie
> When we see not Thro' the Eye
> Which was born in a Night
> To perish in a Night
> When the Soul slept in Beams of Light.
> —William Blake, "Auguries of
> Innocence"

Matt Morrison, Ph.D.
Professor of Rhetoric and Public Address
Abilene Christian University

WORKS CITED

Aristotle. *Rhetoric.* Trans. W. Rhys Roberts. New York: Random House, 1954.

Arnheim, Rudolf. *Visual Thinking.* London: Faber and Faber Limited, 1969.

Budge, Sir E. A. Wallis. *Egyptian Language: Easy Lessons in Egyptian Hieroglyphics.* New York: Dover Books, 1983.

Campbell, George. *The Philosophy of Rhetoric*. ed. Lloyd Bitzer. Carbondale: Southern Illinois University Press, 1963.

Cooper, Lane. *The Rhetoric of Aristotle*. New York: Appleton-Century-Crofts, Inc., 1960.

Lefevre, Carl A. *Linguistics and the Teaching of Reading*. New York: McGraw-Hill Book Co., 1964.

Marcus, Griel. *Mystery Train*. New York: E.P. Dutton, 1975.

Naremore, Rita C., and Robert Hopper. *Children Learning Language*. New York: Harper & Row, 1990.

Peterson, James R. "Eyes Have They, But They See Not." *Psychology Today*. June 1972.

Shahn, Ben. *The Shape of Content*. New York: Vantage Books, 1957.

Turnbull, Andrew, ed. *The Letters of F. Scott Fitzgerald*. New York: Charles Scribner's Sons, 1963, cited by David Herbert Donald. *Look Homeward: A Life of Thomas Wolfe*. Boston: Little, Brown and Company, 1987, 240-241.

Wolfe, Thomas. *Look Homeward, Angel*. New York: Charles Scribner's Sons, 1929.

WORKS CONSULTED

Creber, J. W. Patrick. *Sense and Sensitivity: The Philosophy and Practice of English Teaching*. London: University of London Press, 1965.

Davies, Paul. *The Cosmic Blueprint: New Discoveries in Nature's Creative Ability to Order the Universe*. New York: Simon and Schuster, 1988. In denying the work of God the Creator, Davies is driven to the incredible assertion that "nature organizes itself in such a way as to make the universe self-aware" (163).

Dobie, J. Frank. *The Voice of the Coyote*. Boston: Little, Brown and Company, 1950. Much of the content of my coyote lesson is from this classic.

Edwards, Betty. *Drawing on the Artist Within*. New York: Simon and Schuster, 1986. Edwards says that drawing is a parallel language to reading and the two share the same perceptual heuristics. I go beyond that to assert that art is an energizing quintuplet to *all of the language arts*, and as such should be integrated in instruction as a true basic skill.

Healy, Jane M. *Endangered Minds: Why Our Children Don't Think*. New York: Simon and Schuster, 1990. Healy applies the theory of neural plasticity. She claims that the television age with its hurry-up culture has produced a generation of American children with "two-minute minds." She quotes one teacher: "I feel like kids have one foot out the door on whatever they're doing"(14). Healy lays much of the blame on video games and *Sesame Street*, the "seductive school of organized silliness."

Langer, Susanne K. *Philosophy in a New Key: A Study in the Symbolism of Reason, Rite and Art*. New York: The New American Library, Inc., 1951.

McCarthy, Bernice. *The 4MAT System: Teaching to Learning Styles with Right/Left Mode Techniques*. Barrington, IL: EXCEL, Inc., 1987. This is the most clear and practical application of the extensive research on dual brain function that I have seen. There are two key differences, McCarthy says, in how we learn: "The first is how we *perceive*, the second is how we *process*" (3). The movement through the major learning style dimensions, she says, is the learning process itself: "The movement is from experiencing, to reflecting, to conceptualizing, to tinkering and problem solving, to integrating new learning into the self" (60). Educators and students may contact McCarthy through the publisher: 200 W. Station St., Barrington, IL 60010.

Rico, Gabriele Lusser. *Writing the Natural Way*. Los Angeles: J.P. Tarcher, Inc., 1983. Rico demonstrates how *clustering*, as a key strategy in writing instruction, can be used in "orchestrating hemispheric cooperation" (71-73).

Turbayne, Colin Murray. *The Myth of Metaphor*. Columbia: University of South Carolina Press, 1971.

Questions

1. What does the author mean by, "All learning begins with seeing"?

2. In your study of the gospels, do you see any dominant conversational characteristics of Jesus? What words would you use to describe these features? What scriptures are the most helpful?

3. Tell about a history or English class that appealed to your eyes.

4. Write a poem that appeals to your sense of seeing.

5. Write or tell a familiar Bible story in a way that appeals to the eye and ear.

4

Literature and Moral Education

In 15 years of teaching English at ACU, I've seen the same fundamental question come around many times: how can every department teach its subject in a "Christian" fashion? Is there such a thing as teaching "Christian mathematics"? How can one teach "Christian computer science"? And so on. It's the one faculty-wide discussion from which the English department always emerges smiling. Classes on literature are full of opportunities to discuss authors' values and suggest Christian responses to a text. They may include religious works by Milton, Donne, Tennyson, Buechner, or Walker Percy, or anti-religious works by Sartre, Camus, or Beckett—since either type of work lets the teacher discuss Christian moral issues with the students. Literature courses can even be focused thematically to raise students' consciousness on certain moral issues—ecology, racism, democracy, business ethics, sexism, and so on. Composition classes can include discussion on moral issues. Even workshops in creative writing, being as much a study of human consciousness as of structure, style, and characterization, come naturally to discussions of poets', novelists', and dramatists' world views.

Our experience at church-related colleges is not the only evidence that literature can promote moral education. Writers from Plato to Bacon to Newman to Solzhenitsyn have remarked the influence of literature on character. Even Nikita Khrushchev described writers as "engineers of the human soul" because of the usefulness of literature to Soviet discipline (Charlton 39).

What remains to be said, then, about using literature to promote the moral education of students? What remains is that it can be done very well or very badly. Tonight I bring four proposals to help us do it well. These proposals deal both with the aims of the classroom and with the aims of a lifetime.

My first proposal is that we teach literature so that students can take certain skills *beyond* literature. This mission does not take away the English teacher's traditional mission—helping students enjoy literature for its own sake. I only concede that most students will not take literature as a lifetime hobby. As C. S. Lewis pointed out, most people are "unliterary." They read efficiently and impatiently, either for information or fast-paced entertainment (2-3). And they will always be the majority. Agreeing with Lewis that literature is not the chief end of man, I have reached a "live-and-let-live" attitude toward the unliterary. If they come within my classroom, I will try to win them over to literature. I will use a teacher's passion, personality, and guile to *woo* them to love literature. But if they don't, we will still part as friends. If the unliterary will excuse me from their favorite activities—say, parachute-jumping, preparing my own income tax, or eating sushi—I will excuse them from adoring Shakespeare.

With that issue of *detente* settled, let me argue for making academic skills transferable. The very reading skills that increase our pleasure in a literary work and our understanding of its era are skills that will serve us in society all our lives. If our students can analyze a character in a play, they can one day analyze a candidate in an election; if they can examine an argument in a classroom essay, they can one day evaluate a lawyer's argument as they sit on a jury; if they can ponder the decisions of characters in *Middlemarch, Huckleberry Finn, and The Great Gatsby*, they can better ponder their own decisions in marriage, in friendship, and in careers.

But these are truisms. English teachers either pagan or Christian will probably not argue against teaching these skills. But there is another and more comprehensive skill that the Christian teacher *must* promote as part of education: the ability to detect the *world view* of a book, movie, song, poem, television program, or other artifact. Christians need this skill because of the temperament of modern times and the moral influence of what people consider mere entertainment. The hazards were stated in 1932 by the critic T. S. Eliot. As he wrote in his essay "Religion and Literature," "Secularism" is what motivates governments and authors around the planet, and it gives rise to literature that "repudiates, or is wholly ignorant of, our most fundamental and important [Christian] beliefs." We escape the "degrading" influence of contemporary literature by staying "conscious of the gulf fixed between ourselves" and it. To think of a novel as mere entertainment, to read it passively, is to forget the gulf between its world view and the Christian world view (Ryken 154, 150, 153).

After 50 years, Eliot's advice is still sound. It only needs extension to movies, television, rock videos, beer commercials, and talk-show hosts. The best tool I have found for extending Eliot's advice is a textbook by James W. Sire, *How to Read Slowly: A Christian Guide to Reading with the Mind*. He advises students to "read world-viewishly," staying alert to a literary work's assumptions about human nature, history, free will, and the supernatural.

Eliot and Sire both stress that the Christian answer to literary secularism is *not* to give up reading but to read with more intelligence and care. Students need to hear that advice and make it a policy for the rest of their lives. The problem is not that they'll graduate from college and start reading Hemingway, Lawrence, Dreiser, and other great Moderns whose work may have worried Eliot. The glee with which they sell back their textbooks suggests that they will not be reading the Great Moderns unless at gunpoint. But they may, one of these years, be out at the mall picking up books by Raymond Carver, Joyce Carol Oates, Larry McMurtry, or even Barbara Cartland. Will they be conscious of the gulf between these writers' world views and a Christian world view? Or will they think they're only purchasing "entertainment" and that entertainment cannot affect them?

Will they have a Christian wariness of movies and television? I am not arguing that people have to restrict themselves to Benji or reruns of *The Donna Reed Show* in order to guard their souls. I do want them to transfer what they learned in English, sociology, Bible, communication, and history, and be ready to analyze and weigh what they see. I want them to have a serious reflection or two after watching *Falcon Crest* or Stephen Boccho's latest successor to *Hill Street Blues* and *St. Elsewhere*. This is where the phrase "moral education" needs italics for the word *education*. It does not take much education to be morally disgusted at the idea of an X-rated movie or a topless bar or heavy-metal Satanism or the top-40 song "I Want Your Sex" by British pop star George Michael. It does take education (formal or informal) to detect the more subtle hazard, the world view that is benign but still nonChristian.

For an extended example, let me draw from popular culture rather than literature: I want our students' world-view-detectors turned up fully when they enter Walt Disney World. Yes, friends, the study of literature equips you to read entire theme parks. Our family went to Florida one summer and bought the four-day passes to Epcot Center and the Magic Kingdom. We were not only entertained, we were taught about everything from national polity to drip irrigation. Animated figures of the American presidents taught us the majesty of the U.S. Constitution. Hundreds of singing, spinning marionette children taught us that "It's a Small World After All." The World of Energy pavilion sponsored by Exxon taught us that nuclear generating plants are safe and necessary. A bearded magician and his pet purple dragon taught us that everyone possesses Imagination and that Imagination is what makes us happy and prosperous. The World of Motion pavilion sponsored by General Motors told us that "If we can dream it, we can do it."

In four days at Walt Disney World, I saw only two images of Christianity that were not connected with the Christmas ornament shop. One was of monks in a scriptorium (part of a history of communication). The other was a 30-second shot of a cathedral procession in Montreal, presented, with no comment from the narrator, in a documentary on Canada. Beyond that, the only religious images were little statues of the Buddha in the China pavilion. The sacred text for Walt Disney World turned out to be the valiant little phrase from General Motors: "If we can dream it, we can do it." That phrase echoed in my mind all the way back to Texas. A bit of scripture echoes there, too, the one from Genesis about the tower of Babel—"Come, let us build ourselves a city, with a tower that reaches to the heavens" (11:4). If we can dream it, we can do it!

At Walt Disney World, man is the measure of all things. There is limitless room for the human imagination but no room for the supernatural. I doubt that most tourists are conscious of this world view. Being on vacation, why should they feel analytical? Besides, Disney humanism is like the food in the Disney World restaurants—wholesome, plentiful, nothing bizarre or spicy—acceptable to everybody. Being connected with American individualism, free enterprise, and democracy, the Disney world view is at least as sane and beneficial as those of the Boy Scouts, Girl Scouts, and Rotarians. But it isn't Christianity. Would your own students be alert to it? After shaking hands with Mickey and Goofy, would they begin picking up the ethical and political signals that blink out of every Disney World exhibit? Could they draw on the interpretive skills they've learned in English and other courses?

My second proposal is to promote exchange around that vast, motley clan we might call the Christian *literati*, that is, Christians interested in journalism, communication, literature, or homiletics. The people who like to use their minds, who still have all their old college textbooks, who belong to a Great Books discussion group, who write the occasional item for the church bulletin—these people need to be part of our network as much as the professors of English, Bible, communication, and journalism. The more church leaders who are included, the better.

It seems to me that there's too little community and too little information among Christian readers. Too few are aware of sources and organizations such as the Conference on Christianity and Literature. This group has over 1,500 members across America, most of them professors or writers, from dozens of denominations. They publish a valuable journal, *Christianity and Literature*, and have stimulating national and regional conventions. There is a similar group in England. Besides an awareness of resources, we need a loose "readers' network" of preachers, elders, teachers, editors, writers, general readers, and so on. This network could spread information about conferences such as this one or CCL meetings or Christian-oriented writers' workshops. It would help identify personnel for literary discussion groups and speeches at Christian college lectureships, the Christian Scholars Conference, and other such gatherings. Another thing we need is more space for Christian reviews of books and movies. *Christian Chronicle* and *Christianity Today*, for example, run some fine reviews but can't begin to meet the need. The book review editor for *Christian Chronicle* will soon be limiting reviews to 100-150 words so that more can be run in each issue. Publishers keep churning out books, and Christian readers are calling more and more frequently for informed opinions about those books.

My third proposal is that more Christian professors of English become up-to-date in their practice of moral education through literature. Too many haven't moved past about 1960 in their conception of teaching English. I confess that my own notions solidified about 1979, the year I finished my doctorate. Like most professors, we were trained mostly by example. We do about what our own professors did when we were students. What's good is that we've resisted most pedagogical fads. What's bad is that many of us are unaware of developments in literary criticism, some of them dangerous and some of them helpful. By ignoring recent Marxist critics or deconstruction-ists, for example, we may also ignore their opponents—our own potential allies.

I will give only one example of recent developments that our Christian colleagues may overlook, a flamboyantly antireligious article by deconstructionist critic Jonathan Culler in *Profession 86*, published by the Modern Language Association. Culler calls for "antireligious satire to keep the sanctimonious in check" and complains that "Comparative literature grows pious and works to legitimate rather than criticize and situate religious discourse" (31). Temperamentally, my colleagues and I are "Old Paths" people. We feel secure teaching the same classics year after year and ignoring critical movements and fads. But when secularism has such brilliant advocates as Jonathan Culler, Stanley Fish, and other deconstructionists, it's time we all listened.

My last proposal is to give special training to our future "professionals"—the Bible, English, and communication majors—who are likely to create or review or teach works of literature, TV, or film. I don't restrict this proposal to students at the Christian colleges. We need a network that includes students at state universities and in university ministries at congregations across the country. If we can locate these future professionals, we can cultivate them by sending summaries about conferences like this, giving them subscriptions to journals such as *Christianity and Literature*, starting a newsletter with a readers' forum in which they could participate, or setting up a lending library for audio or video cassettes.

I'll conclude with news items. Some projects are already underway to build literary awareness among members of the churches of Christ. One is the day-long writing conference at Northeastern Christian College a few years ago, in which guest writers discussed professional matters *and* their Christian vocation in writing. Another is in the planning by James Thompson, Doug Cragg, and Robert Reynolds at the Institute of Christian Studies. They hope to bring a well-know writer to Austin next spring to hold a forum on writing and Christianity. The most comprehensive new project is the Center for Christian Writing, sponsored by the English department at ACU. Using the network we already have with colleagues at Harding, Oklahoma Christian, Lipscomb, and the other Christian schools, we hope to promote community among Christian readers and writers. For example, we plan to have a visiting speaker on Christian fiction next spring. For the 1989 Bible Lectureship at ACU, three colleagues involved in the Center are giving a series entitled "The Battle for the Mind: Secularism and Modern Literature." Before too long, we hope to start a network of readers and writers such as I've described. Step one will be to have a student worker raid a couple of prominent Rolodexes and type the addresses into our computer.

So far, this Center for Christian Writing is mostly a collection of modest ideas. We have studied the Christian literary institutes at Wheaton College and at Friends University, and we think the time is right to render our fellowship the same kind of service they render to theirs. If you're interested in the project, we'd be glad to have your name and address.

Let me sum up these 20 minutes' ponderings on literature and moral education. There is an inescapable relation between them. Literature *will* affect a reader's moral perceptions inside or outside a classroom. So will film and television. It falls to us—professors, ministers, parents, preachers, interested parties—to make the mechanism plain to students. We have to convince them of the moral power of literature and film if we hope to educate them for a lifetime as Christian readers and spectators. It can be a worrisome enterprise, but it's always vital and often exciting.

Chris Willerton, Ph.D.
Professor of English
Director of the Honors Program
Abilene Christian University
A paper delivered at the Christian Scholars
Conference,
> *Pepperdine University, 21 July 1988*

Works Cited

Charlton, James, ed. *The Writer's Quotation Book: A Literary Companion.* Rev. ed. [New York]: Pushcart, 1985.

Culler, Jonathan. "Comparative Literature and the Pieties." *Profession 86*, 30-32. For a reply, see Roy Battenhouse, "Anti-Religion in Academia." *Christianity and Literature*, 37.1 (1987), 7-22.

Lewis, C. S. *An Experiment in Criticism.* 1961. Rep. London: Cambridge UP, 1965.

Ryken, Leland, ed. *The Christian Imagination: Essays on Literature and the Arts.* Grand Rapids: Baker, 1981.

Sire, James W. *How to Read Slowly: A Christian Guide to Reading with the Mind.* Downers Grove, IL: InterVarsity, 1978.

Questions

1.   What does the author mean by "world view"?

2.   From the list below select one item and explain the world view which is presented.
     Star Wars trilogy
     Indiana Jones trilogy
     Field of Dreams
     The Cosby Show
     The Simpsons

3.   The essay discusses the influence of secular literature and media on society. Give one positive example and one negative example of the influence of literature/media on you and your friends.

4.   The essay discusses the philosophy that views "man as the measure of all things." How can this view negatively affect your faith?

5

Some Perspectives on Practical Biology

O n the opening day of class the instructor said, "OK, students, today and for the rest of the semester we'll be looking at organisms (mostly dead and preserved in buckets at the back of the room) and classify them according to

kingdom
 phylum
  class
   order
    family
     genus
      species."

Talk about a way to kill enthusiasm on the first day of the semester!

For many students this is what "biology" brings to mind, along with having to do an insect collection and dissecting dead frogs. While I agree that scientific classification of organisms is an important tool for professional biologists and that the study of frog anatomy is fascinating and informative, a typical student, including maybe you, logically asks, "What does that have to do with me?"

In contrast, consider two recent articles in the *Journal of the American Medical Association* (*JAMA*, as those in the know seem to call it) and *Sports Illustrated*. *JAMA* published an unsigned and supposedly unsolicited four-paragraph article entitled "It's over, Debbie." This article was an account of a gynecology resident physician awakened during the night, called to the side of a 20-year-old female dying of ovarian cancer. She seems to be in great pain and near death and seems, to the physician, to request euthanasia, that is, mercy killing. The physician complies with this request by injecting her with a fatal dose of morphine.

The publishing of that article prompted significant comment from the readership of *JAMA* (as well as those outside) and the magazine devoted ten pages of a subsequent edition to publishing selected letters to the editor and more extended commentaries on the article. Responses ranged from thoughtful praise of the physician to calls for his/her arrest for pre-meditated murder.

About the same time *Sports Illustrated* published a rather long article entitled "Competition." In this article the writer attempted to analyze the role of competition in American society. The focus was on sports competition, but there was liberal space devoted to the apparent basic competitive nature of humans, the effects of that nature on relationships and business, and the role of human biology in that nature.

These articles, as well as many others, identify an aspect of biology which is much more practical to most people, an aspect which does and will require Christian decisions in situations which may not be centrally biological, but have a strong biology flavor to them. It is my contention that the more biology a person knows, the more informed decisions one can make.

We don't hear the term "situation ethics" used all that much these days, but the idea is still around and touches ethical concerns with which we must wrestle. I'm sure it is a simplification, but the idea here implies to me that each situation is unique and therefore there are no general principles which can serve as guides. Certainly, there are different bioethical situations arising every week, it seems, and we need to give each individual consideration. But an overemphasis on the variety and uniqueness (of which there is much) must not blind us to the fact that many of these bioethical situations *do* have a common thread which can be considered, even *before* the situation is encountered.

On the other hand, though we should search for and cherish these underlying principles and values, exclusive attention to principles can result in a pattern of legalism and instances where we lose our ability to function as servants of God. This we must guard against also.

But maybe I'm getting ahead of myself. The point is, there are many current problems of medicine, aging, food distribution, use of natural resources, and so on, which represent practical biology and they are a long way from

kingdom
    phylum
        class
           order
                family

genus

species.

It is important as Christians to understand that these bioethical situations, many of which are quite troubling, need a response. Each of us lives in a body which may be healthy now, but will not always be so; and those we love live in the same kind of bodies. Furthermore, Jesus taught us to be "givers of cups of cold water." How can we do this in a world beset with such difficult dilemmas as starving populations, abortions, and genetic engineering?

Each of you reading is at least somewhat familiar with the topics of concern. And you probably share the feeling which many of us have, a feeling of despair because the problems seem so large and unsolvable. But the scriptures indicate that believers are to be an aid to those with little hope, so we *must* dive in and see what we can do.

A good friend of mine once suggested that there are some problems which we never will be able to solve as humans, but that we can whittle them away a little bit. He was discussing the book of Job and the problem of suffering, but the advice applies to the "practical" biology topics, too. We may not be able to reach a conclusion which will make these very rough spots smooth, but perhaps, with God's help, we can whittle away at the problem, sharpen the focus some so we can, at least, clearly see the problem and the options available to us.

Biology is the study of life. In a general biology class one usually discusses what it means to be "alive." Something which is alive is described as having certain characteristics such as the ability to reproduce, an awareness and responsiveness to its environment, a host of biochemical reactions resulting in oxygen consumption, for example, plus a couple of other attributes. Studying the part of creation involving living things, standing in awe at the wonder and intricacies of life—this must be one of the greatest pleasures of a Christian biologist. I would suggest that this point of wonder at life should be the thesis statement as we grapple with these hard problems which have biology implications.

But sometimes the water gets murky. Sometimes it is obvious that all life does not seem to be equivalent. Sometimes we have to kill other organisms, to take away the very gift for which we are thankful.

In a heart transplant situation a *live* heart is removed from a *dead* (or dying?) body and placed in another body which would die more rapidly without the replacement heart. It is clear that the good heart has a life of its own in a sense which is different from the life of the donor. Life would appear to exist on different levels within one organism.

Furthermore, the lives of different organisms seem to vary in value. Once I gave students what is called the "hammer test." In this exercise the students were given a rather long list of organisms (plant, animal, and microorganism) along with a hypothetical hammer. The students were told they could hammer (and therefore kill) any individual organism on the list as long as they had a good enough reason. The students were happily in agreement to hammer such organisms as tapeworms and the bacterium which causes strep throat, but disagreement arose over bluebirds, deer, lions, and humans. I think you can see the problem: what is a good enough reason for one person to kill is insufficient for someone else. Is it possible that God wants us to believe life is sacred but that it is also acceptable to kill (even other humans) at times *without* violating that sacredness?

It is on this particular "sacredness of life" idea that bioethical issues rotate. If we believe that life is important, we are forced to make several difficult choices to nurture and sustain it at times, and to end it at other times.

This does sound different from stale biology, doesn't it?

A few examples might clarify this point. For the past 40 years molecular genetics has been one of the dominant sub-fields of biology. The explanation of deoxyribonucleic acid (DNA) as the genetic material carrying hereditary information plus subsequent understanding of cellular genetics have led us into the era of genetic engineering. Experiments have now been done in which hereditary characteristics have been added to organisms which originally lacked those characteristics. Although the difficulties of such manipulations with humans are great, they do not look impossible for the future. Altering the genetic capability of an individual (human or otherwise) is a significant biologic move and shows great promise in such areas as increasing crop yields and improving livestock, as well as medical uses for genetic deficiencies of humans. But the mention of "genetic deficiencies" implies that a judgement will have to be made as to what characteristics *are* "deficiencies."

On a related topic, problems of infertile couples have taken on new dimensions with the availability of artificial insemination, sperm banks, and surrogate motherhood. The problems here get sticky fast. If a woman is artificially inseminated by sperm from a male not her husband (because her husband is infertile), who is the father of the child? If a female can produce eggs but cannot carry a fetus for nine months without endangering her own (and its) life, so the fertilized egg is implanted into another female, who is the mother? If the sperm from a male are mixed with eggs from a female to insure fertilization occurring, probably only one would be implanted back into the female to mature. What is to become of the *other* fertilized eggs which have now probably divided a few times and are small clusters of human tissue (or are they human beings? or *potential* human beings?)

The "family" would seem to be an important unit in Christian belief; both physical and spiritual families are addressed in scripture. New fertilization techniques, however, are disturbing the traditional family unit as we have known it and may force us to clarify family composition. What will be the definition of a parent? It would appear that it will be possible to separate the "biology" of parenthood from the caretaker, nurturer, and loving support aspect of being a parent. Child welfare and adoption workers already wrestle daily with such dimensions, and there must be a call for clear Christian thinking here.

The question of abortion fits here, of course, too. Is killing ever justified? What is killed in an abortion? Is there some scriptural help available? Get out your Bible and read some of the passages said, by some, to address the issue (Exodus 21:22-25; Psalms 139:13-18; Jeremiah 1:4-6; Job 10:10-13). What is God telling you in these passages?

I believe it is important to do at least two things here. One is to refrain from drawing battle lines too rigidly. Conscientious, caring Christians differ on when, if ever, abortion should be an option. We need to be supportive as well as instructive to one another on these hard decisions. Second, we need to remember that life is important and should never be dealt with trivially, no matter what scale of life we are considering.

I would leave these life/death issues with only passing references to at least two other related ideas, hunting for sport and the use of experimental animals in scientific research.

Can we justify killing something for fun? Can we justify killing something for fun if we then eat it? Game management may very well depend on killing back a herd, but what does that say about an individual getting pleasure from having an animal in the gun sight?

Many advances in medicine have occurred because experimental animals were used as test models. Most people would agree that such animal use is justified, but there have been, clearly, some abuses of animals, situations where the well-being and the life of the animal have been seen as insignificant.

Let me take a break from these examples to remind you, the reader, what the goal of all this is. I contend that there are many events of modern (and future) life which have a biologic aspect to them and that these events are best considered from a broad informational base. The more we know about a problem, the more accurately we will address it. We need smart, Christian biologists doing this research, manning the committees, and serving the patients, and we need smart, Christian citizens supporting issues and candidates and working through their own personal bioethical situations.

As a final example of a tangled problem requiring clear, Christian thinking, I would use an article published in the late 1960s by a California biologist, Garrett Hardin. Although as a Christian I have large problems with some of Hardin's ideas, this article, "The Tragedy of the Commons," made a profound point to me.

The thesis of Hardin's article can best be summarized by adapting one of his examples. Suppose there was a large pasture and ten herdsmen were using it cooperatively. Each herdsman had ten animals in the field and, since none of the ten individuals owned the field, they used it in "common" (it was a "commons"). One of the herdsmen realizes that if he places an eleventh animal on the field he will get more profit; it is true that his other ten animals will have less to eat, but this shortage will be spread across the other nine herdsmen. Since he stands to gain more than he loses, he adds animal number eleven. All the other herdsmen have the same thought, of course. Soon each one has eleven animals on the commons. Each herdsman then realizes that, by placing a twelfth animal on the field, he will profit more than he will be hurt. Soon each herdsman has twelve animals on the commons.

Hardin suggests that this trend of adding animals will continue until, finally, the field is overgrazed and the commons disappears. The driving force behind this "tragedy of the commons" was each herdsman's individual greed and lack of foresight.

The article continues, then, by pointing out that we live in a world of "commons," and that it is important to recognize the role of greed in ruining commons. For example, the total food production capability of the world represents a commons and we need to recognize that anyone or any nation taking more than its "share" is taking advantage of the commons. The amount of oil reserves in the world represents a commons. The time of a teacher in a crowded classroom represents a commons and a child demanding an extra amount of that time is infringing on the commons.

The commons idea is simplistic in a way but does, to me, have a Christian ring to it. If we are to be bearing cups of cold water, if we are to be touching physical lives so we can share spiritual light, we need to be filled with compassion and counter greed and selfishness where it rises. As Christians we are very aware of our finiteness and that we live in a world of finite quantities, including time. We need to get on with our mission.

In closing, I suspect that you may not have agreed with all that I have said. Or you may have "read between the lines" and found something with which to disagree. That's ok with me.

I have tried to touch on some hard problems. These problems are not just biological; they are often political/sociological/religious/economic/biological. These are challenging times to be a student. These are especially challenging times to be a Christian student. Integrating frighteningly new information with solid historic truths requires study, compassion, good will, and insight from God.

James R. Nichols, Ph.D.
Professor of Biology
Abilene Christian University

Questions

1. What sources (i.e., friends, specific scriptures, laws) would you use to guide your decisions about the following:
   • Can we justify killing something for fun?
   • Can we justify killing something for fun if we eat it?

2. Put yourself in the same situation as the students who were given the "hammer test." What choices would you make? Explain your rationale.

3. Is it possible that God wants us to believe life is sacred but that it is also acceptable to kill (even other humans) at times without violating that sacredness? Explain your position.

4. The essay states that we live in a world of "commons," and that "it is important to recognize the role of greed in ruining commons." Relate two specific examples that demonstrate this principle.

5. How can the study of biology help you make important moral choices?

6

The Need for Servant Leaders

When most of us are informed that the need in our world is for more servants, our mental picture is of a slave. Someone who is stooped, subservient, compliant. One who is under some master authority. The idea is repugnant to us.

"Who me, a servant?" you ask. "You have got to be kidding! Why would I want to be anybody's *slave?*"

Yet if you are to be effective in leadership for today, it will be because you have learned to serve. Joseph Shulum from Jerusalem, Israel, tells the story of a rabbi's son who had severe emotional problems. The boy went into the back yard, stripped himself of his clothing, then crouched down and gobbled like a turkey. This behavior continued for several weeks, and though many of the rabbi's friends offered either remedies or sympathy, nothing changed for the boy.

Finally a friend came who said he believed he could help. He warned the rabbi not to be alarmed by his methods, but to let him try to reach the son. Assured of the father's support, the friend went into the back yard and imitated the son's behavior. They both assumed the crouched position and gobbled as turkeys do. After several days of this way of acting, the friend asked, "Do you think it would be alright for turkeys to wear shirts?"

The boy agreed, and they each put on a shirt. Then the friend inquired, "Would it be alright to wear trousers?" Again the boy agreed. They also began to stand erect, and not crouched. Little by little the friend talked to the boy and demonstrated to him his loving concern. And as they talked, the boy's sanity returned and he was able, finally, to rejoin his father in a new and meaningful way of living.

In a similar way, Jesus came to the earth to find a "bunch of turkeys" who had lost their way. He stripped himself of his royal robes and began to make himself like us. He emptied himself of glory and took "the very nature of a servant" (Philippians 2:7). He chose a strange but compelling way to teach us—that of a servant.

The Lesson Jesus Taught

Over and over Jesus demonstrated and explained what servant leadership is all about. This teaching was to his chosen men, the apostles. Often we have the idea that they were great spiritual giants, and that you and I could never attain such maturity. Yet the gospel record shows us just the opposite. They were very slow to learn servanthood, perhaps because that is not the way the world thinks.

On the road to Capernaum once, these men argued about who was the greatest. This sounds familiar to our ears too. We still concern ourselves with who is great or who has power and prestige. We argue the merits of one student over another for a class office or an honor. Deep down in your innermost heart, you know that you may not be *the* greatest but you do not want to be the *least*. So the struggle within goes on to make a place for oneself, to be known by name by others, to achieve some kind of recognition.

Jesus first told the Twelve, "If anyone wants to be first, he must be the very last, and the *servant of all*" (Mark 9:35). Then he used a child as an object lesson, placing him in the midst of these self-seeking, feuding men and announced, "Whoever welcomes one of these little children in my name welcomes me" (Mark 9:37). The real lesson for you to remember is that unless we take on the attributes of a child—humility, forgiveness, love and compassion—you cannot even hope to enter the kingdom of heaven!

On another occasion, James and John asked for the chief seats in Christ's coming kingdom. They wanted to sit to the right and left of their leader, comparable to our Secretary of State and Secretary of the Treasury. They were rather bold in their requests, thinking perhaps that if the seats of honor were granted to them they would be truly great. You can imagine the reaction of the ten remaining apostles—they were indignant! So many people in our world want to be "Top Dog" that they claw their way in life seeking for greatness. Yet Jesus spoke words to his disciples that are still very applicable to us and our situation.

> You know that those who are regarded as rulers of the Gentiles lord it over them, and their high officials exercise authority over them. Not so with you. Instead, whoever wants to be great among you must be your servant, and whoever wants to be first must be slave of all. For even the Son of Man did not come to be served, but to serve, and to give His life a ransom for many. (Mark 10:42-45)

The way up is the way down—learning to be a servant. Once someone asked Leonard Bernstein what was the hardest instrument to play in the orchestra. Without hesitation he replied, "Second fiddle." He then explained, "In all my years of working with orchestras I have never had anyone tell me that they played second, third or fourth chair, but always first chair, whatever their instrument was. Yet unless we have people who are willing to play in a lesser position, the orchestra would never be able to make beautiful harmony."

Service. That is the ticket to greatness. We need to imitate Jesus in serving others rather than being served.

At the last supper, we again find these disciples of Jesus in a dispute over which of them was the greatest. Most of the time you and I are "turned off" by people who self-proclaim their accomplishments, awards and opinions on everything, leaving us with the undeniable feeling they know how great they are. We even wonder if they take the "I" vitamin!

It really seems incongruous that when Jesus met with his disciples in the upper room that they would be fussing over something so trivial as human greatness and position. So Jesus has to instruct them once more in where true greatness lies. "Instead, the greatest among you should be like the youngest, and the one who rules like the one who serves. For who is greater, the one who is at the table or the one who serves? Is it not the one who is at the table? But I am among you as one who serves" (Luke 22:26-27).

The Lesson Jesus Demonstrated
In this context of the last supper, just hours before the cross, Jesus decided to demonstrate what it meant to be a servant both for His men and for all of us. Maybe He decided that it took more than mere telling; He would have

to show servanthood. John is the only writer who depicts it
for us in his gospel account.

> Jesus knew that the Father had put all things
> under His power, and that He had come from
> God and was returning to God; so He got up
> from the meal, took off His outer clothing, and
> wrapped a towel around His waist. After that,
> He poured water into a basin and began to
> wash His disciples' feet, drying them with the
> towel that was wrapped around Him.
> When He had finished washing their feet, He
> put on His clothes and returned to His place.
> "Do you understand what I have done for
> you?" He asked them. "You call Me 'Teacher'
> and 'Lord,' and rightly so, for that is what I
> am. Now that I, your Lord and Teacher, have
> washed your feet, you also should wash one
> another's feet. I have set you an example that
> you should do as I have done for you. I tell
> you the truth, no servant is greater than his
> master, nor is a messenger greater than the
> one who sent him. Now that you know these
> things, you will be blessed if you do them.
> (John 13:3-5, 12-17)

Each disciple of Jesus must have thought within his
own heart that he was an invited guest to the supper.
Where was a servant to do the customary washing of their
feet? They each knew one thing: it is not my place to wash
anyone's feet. How surprised they all must have been when
their Teacher started doing this menial task. Jesus was
actually washing their feet! He powerfully showed them
what kind of leader He was—as servant. There are a
number of parallel lessons for us, as well.

He got up from the meal—as He had left His throne in glory.

He took off His outer garment—as He had divested Himself of godlikeness.

He wrapped a towel around His waist—as He had wrapped Himself in our humanity.

He poured water into a basin and begin to wash the disciples' feet—as He died to bring us cleansing and forgiveness.

He dried their feet with a towel—even as His humanity was put at their disposal.

He set the example that we should wash one another's feet—and thus opened the way of blessing for us.

The Application

The disciples wanted a *Title*. Instead, Jesus gave a *towel*. They missed the point of servanthood, and so often do we. When we are consumed with self, we will behave as if the whole scheme of redemption was for us alone. We get to thinking all of this was done to make us feel good and to get things going our way.

Yet the One they called Lord and Teacher was a servant. He took the lowliest of tasks, stooping down to wash the disciples' feet. Servanthood is quiet and unannounced as Jesus began doing what the others thought ought to be done by someone. Because He washed their feet, He now instructs us to wash one another's feet.

In our day, there may not be many occasions when you or I will literally have to wash someone's feet. But if we are perceptive and sensitive to others' needs, there will be countless opportunities for service. The world cries out for people who surrender selfishness and choose to serve. Your life will be a blessing to others when you serve in the varied ways that come up each day. Your life will be blessed more because you serve others than by waiting for someone to serve you.

The song that young people often sing has the right spirit and should be put into practice.

Make me a servant, Lord,
Make me like You.
For you are a servant,
Make me one too.

The world needs such servants. Colleges and universities need these servants. Businesses long for those whose interests are for others in ways they can serve them. Congregations crave for servant-leaders. In an attempt to identify the kind of personalities that we so eagerly desire, I have put together the following profile:

The Servant Leader Is . . .

- One who can get down on a child's level and listen intently to him.

- An elder who stands at the church house door to speak to the people by name.

- A person who can make you feel that you are not beneath him/her, but gives you an understanding response.

- The friend who came to see you when your mother or father died, and just cried with you.

- The preacher who can speak of his own struggles in his sermons as a way of helping you with yours.

- The lady who takes a pie to a sick

neighbor, and then stays to help clean the house.

- One who invites you into his home and makes you feel part of the family.

- The teacher who genuinely asks, "How are you getting along?"

- The person who sits by you in a strange class and makes you feel welcomed.

- The friend who lovingly can correct you when you are in the wrong.

- The person who goes to the hospital to sit several hours with a patient who needs continuing care.

- The teenager who mows the lawn of the elderly widow.

- The fifth grader who visits the nursing home to see a friend he has made, and takes him some fruit.

- The teacher who gives a child in her classroom a Bible storybook as a special treat for a birthday.

- The deacon who takes off a week from work to help anyway he is needed in Christian Youth Camp.

- The Christian who goes on a campaign for Christ in another culture and works to truly know and relate to the people.

- The person who speaks to everyone he/she meets, calling out, "It's good to see you!"

- One who is more anxious to serve others than to be served by them.

Jim Mankin, D.Min.
Associate Professor of Bible
Chairman, Department of Undergraduate
Bible and Ministry
Director, Center for Christian Leadership
Abilene Christian University

Questions

1. Compare and contrast Christian humility and Christian pride.

2. What are some "second fiddle" responsibilities in the kingdom that the kingdom cannot do without?

3. What situations today would be comparable to washing feet?

4. *Time/Life* selects the top ten people of the century. Select your top five "servant leaders." Explain the criteria you used in making your selections.

5. List at least three service opportunities that you will commit yourself to this month.

7

Researching Romance: One Tie That Binds

s a young teen I began asking adults if they knew where I could find out about men and women. They always nodded knowingly and found me some books about male and female anatomy and pamphlets on sexual ethics. I was always disappointed. I wanted to know about the mysterious, elusive elixir of romance—the alchemy that transformed individuals into loving partners. I was sure it was more than simply hormones coursing through veins and a moral decision about sexual behavior.

After years of study and experience, I still believe the connection between partners—a healthy unity, the "one flesh" that Jesus said was God's original intention—is a great deal more than a good biological match or a social arrangement governed by legal precepts. Love, with its usual intensity, involves more of the self than many of life's experiences. As Christian lovers, we may be physically held, but we are also emotionally held, mentally held, and perhaps spiritually held. Our ideals, our values, those things we most cherish and respect are mirrored in our mutually loving relationships. The idealization or celebration of my loved ones aids me in transforming my dearest values into deeds; indeed, it is often said that what we love ardently determines much of what we become.

The Bible holds haunting images of intimately connected couples, from the Songs of Solomon writer's longing for his beloved to Paul's tender metaphor of the Bride of Christ. The creation story in Genesis speaks of humanity being made in the image of God—"male and female" (Genesis 5:2)—and the reunion possible when the two become "one flesh" (Genesis 2:24). God manifests himself to us as a fluidly dynamic person, wooing and waiting, hiding and revealing, giving and receiving: an ever-changing interplay of polarities. Some Christian writers speak of God's romancing of humanity through the ages; the church in faith awaits the consummation of seeing her Beloved "face to face."

Academic Research on Love

In a classic study, Harry Harlow and Robert Zimmermann demonstrated that infant monkeys spend a great deal more time with a cloth surrogate mother than with a wire surrogate, regardless of which mother provides the milk. They proposed, as have later students of human infants, that the need for "contact comfort" is innate. Soon after, Ferreira concluded from infant research that the need for intimacy is "primary and of an instinctual nature . . . the intimacy need may represent a more basic instinctual force than oral or even nursing needs." Angyal theorized that the establishment and maintenance of a close relationship—and close relationships can include those with friends, children, or spouses—is "the crux of our existence from the cradle to the grave" (19). Erik Erikson proposed the capacity for intimacy which emerges in young adulthood as one of the major developmental tasks of life.

Intimate relationships in adulthood are thought to be an echo of the early attachment of the infant to its caregiver. During the first few months of life, the attachment the infant experiences to the caregiver is unambivalent—that is, the infant very soon begins to reward the approaching caregiver with smiles and reaching gestures, is soothed by the caregiver's presence, and reacts with dismay when the caregiver moves away.

During the second year of life, however, the toddler seems to experience a rising need to experiment with separation and individuation from the caregiver—giving rise to the assertion of independence known as "the terrible two's." At the same time, the young child continues to return to the caregiver and to seek assurance of a strong attachment between them; indeed, the exploration behavior of the toddler appears to be *fostered* by the base of a strong attachment with the caregiver.

Middle childhood is again a time of relatively unambivalent attachment to caregivers while the child explores in widening circles away from home. Early adolescence marks the return of a period of testing the boundaries of those in the caregiving relationship. Thus, from their earliest experiences, human beings move back and forth from separateness and connection, needing both and being satisfied by neither for very long.

The adult version of close connection is often the experience of falling in love. Falling in love and being in love (connecting) is highly valued in American culture—perhaps *because* in the larger scheme we place such a premium value on individuality (separateness). Yet new love's intensity seldom endures more than a few months or years, and as it wanes, many couples question the validity of their relationship.

Other couples discover new satisfactions of intimacy growing to replace the original form of intensity. What follows "falling in love" in loves that endure? Some investigators of love and romance through the life-span find that what usually begins as "passionate love" evolves over time into "companionate love." (Passionate love is characterized by emotional intensity and strong physical attraction; companionate love is the affection we feel for those with whom our lives are deeply intertwined.)

Despite the common-sense sound of these observations, few empirical studies have assessed the developmental progression of the love experience. As late as 1986, one love researcher observed:

> Despite the increasing scientific and public interest in issues of adult development, we continue to have little empirical knowledge of the ways in which contemporary men and women in early adulthood negotiate issues of love and friendship. . . . There is a clear need to investigate the origins and vicissitudes of intimate relationships in young adults. (Raskin 169-170)

One reason for the deficit has been lack of agreement about what love is—is it an emotion (what one feels), an attitude (what one thinks), or a behavior (what one does)? If a theory of love were to be developed and accepted, other questions would still remain: How shall it be measured? How can we construct measures that are accurate and valid? Will they test what we intend?

Love is certainly one of the most elusive and subjective of all experiences. While much remains to be done, the past decade has at least brought the subject respectability as an area of scientific research.

Measuring Romantic Love

Early psychological theories of love describe love as a global or ideal emotion. Attempts at analysis aim at capturing love's *essence*. While our culture does use the word "love" as a broad experience that is similar in a wide variety of circumstances, common sense also points to the fact that even one form of love between partners called "romantic love" can differ markedly from one couple to another, or between the partners within a couple.

To capture this variety in experience, recent research on romantic love distinguishes between aspects of the love experience by proposing that love indeed is a "many-splendored thing." Two general kinds of love are proposed by Walster and Walster, as mentioned above: passionate and companionate. Kelley (1983) adds a model for what he calls "pragmatic love." In a theory linking romantic love and early attachment experiences, Hazen and Shaver (1987) argue that while a "core experience" of love is shared by all, differences in patterns and emphasis show that love is a multidimensional phenomenon, and that individuals differ in more ways than simply the intensity of their love experience.

My own research is based on the notion that "love" has multiple dimensions. I investigate six basic love styles, borrowed from classic conceptions of love, and elaborated by Hendrick and Hendrick: Eros (passionate love), Ludus (game playing love), Storge (friendship love), Pragma (logical, "shopping list" love), Mania (possessive, dependent love) and Agape (all-giving, selfless love). Young single people, my research indicates, have a more "manic" and "ludic" love style than other age groups, while married seniors with children who have left home express the most "agapic" and—interestingly—"erotic" love styles. Contrary to some popular notions, passionate, romantic love does not appear to be the exclusive privilege of the young, but is experienced throughout the lifespan in both old and new relationships.

I find it interesting that while most of the lovestyles vary according to other factors (for example, highly religious people have a more agapic love style, and persons with higher incomes have a less manic love style), eros-love is unaffected by any of the variables included in my study—perhaps evidence of the physiological aspects of love common to all.

The unanswered question at this point is whether the differences I find in love styles are because of changes brought about by age and personal development, changes in the general culture (popular wisdom about relationships is much different in content than it was in the 1950s, when many in the sample initiated their present relationships), or changes due to varying lengths of the respondents' relationships.

Changing Values In The Experience of Romance

Another interesting area of ongoing love research documents current changes in what men and women are experiencing as "romantic." One study (Critelli, Myers & Loos) compared men and women who espoused separate and distinct male and female gender role patterns ("traditionals") with those who evidenced egalitarian and flexible gender role patterns ("nontraditionals") on a measure of love. They found differences between men and women who value sex role polarity and those who do not: "Traditional" men and women feel that romantic dependency ("my love makes life worth living") and romantic compatibility ("my love and I are meant for each other") are the most important aspects of their love, while "nontraditional" men and women feel that communicative intimacy ("my love and I are close friends") is most important.

The debate about what really brings partners together continues. If love and attraction are based on the oppositions between the genders, as many have suggested, our culture has much to fear from the growing reduction of sex role differences. "Women are equal because they are not different any more. . . . The polarity of the sexes is disappearing, and with it erotic love, which is based on this polarity" (Fromm 13). On the other hand, it can be argued that those who have reduced their prescribed role polarization "may be in a better position to understand the opposite sex and develop closer, more loving, less conflictual relationships" (Critelli 364).

One clue to this puzzle is found, interestingly enough, in the scholarly studies of so-called "romance novels." In *Good-bye Heathcliff: Changing Heroes, Heroines, Roles and Values in Women's Category Romances*, Miriam Darce Frenier remarks on the evolving pattern of relationships in these novels as a mirror of contemporary culture. Significant changes, she points out, have occurred in the flavor of the novels which are most popular with consumers. In the 1960s and the 1970s, as the romance genre exploded, spirited heroines were contained by powerful (and sometimes brutal), protective heroes. By the early 1980s the tide had turned in favor of tender, egalitarian heroes and savvy heroines. Another important change occurred in the "glue" that held the hero and heroine together. In older category romances, men and women were opposites; action in the story revolved around their antagonisms and misunderstandings. In the new romances, however, the protagonists are often portrayed as more alike than different. The drama derives from their movement toward understanding themselves and each other, or in uniting their efforts against an external challenge. If this literary trend reflects actual cultural changes, then the cold war between the sexes may be nearing a truce.

Conclusions

To close this brief review, I will offer my integration of researching romance into my larger work of faith.

The Christian word for healing or making whole is *salvation*. Salvation is our hope because we, as human beings, are subject to constant actions, events and interpretations which isolate us from ourselves, each other, and our God. The Healer came to save us and to be a personal example of reaching across the chasms which isolate us. The "second commandment" of loving one's neighbor as oneself indicates God's concern with the quality of our relationships, which surely include those toward whom we feel "romantic."

The exquisite range of emotions which we call love is not only one of God's gifts to us, it is also God's commandment. An eloquent statement on behalf of the "healthiness" of an oft-suspicioned kind of love—eros—is made by John Carmody in his book, *Holistic Spirituality*. He argues covincingly that eros is a "wonderful pain," a longing for union that adds color and depth to the self-sacrificing agapic love highlighted in the New Testament. "What I learn joined to my spouse I shall apply wherever I can," he writes. "The determination my eros gives, its steel for my soul, is a powerful opponent of death. Though the enemies of eros slay me, yet will I trust it, since it is the mark of my God" (96). The mystery of romantic love, when it is not interpreted as simply instincts and hormones or discussions of ethical sexual behavior, hints of the essence of life.

The powerful experience of romantic love impacts the life of an earnest Christian no less than anyone else. It helps us, hinders us, uplifts us, and lets us fall. Sometimes the celebration of the loved person is based on imagination rather than the real qualities of the loved, and the discovery of this can result in profound dismay and disillusionment.

Many of us are uncomfortable with our solitary self, and romantic love can become a flight from our individual responsibility to search for the purpose and meaning of our own life. But romantic love is also a transformative power, and if there is congruity between our spiritual goals and our choice of partners, the act of loving can teach us much about ourselves and our purpose. When celebrating our loved one, we celebrate the gift and goodness of life. We affirm again our vision of what is good—what is Godly—and rededicate ourselves to manifesting good in the world.

In conclusion, then, love is central to our understanding of God. It is the central challenge of life for the Christian. It is also now regarded as an essential area of research in the study of human development. My hope as a academician, and a Christian, is that my science will ever lead me on to new ground from which I can honor Grace.

Marilyn Montgomery McCormick
Department of Human Development and
Family Studies
Texas Tech University

Works Cited

Angyal, A. *Neurosis and Treatment: A Holistic Theory*. New York: John Wiley and Sons, 1965.

Carmody, John. *Holistic Spirituality*. New York: Paulist Press, 1983.

Critelli, Myers, & Loos. "The Components of Love: Romantic Attraction and Sex Role Orientation." *Journal of Personality and Social Psychology*, 54 (1986): 354-370.

Erikson, E. H. *Identity: Youth and Crisis*. New York: Norton, 1968.

Ferreira, A. J. "The Intimacy Need in Psychotherapy." *American Journal of Psychoanalysis*, 24 (1964): 190-194.

Frenier, M. D. *Good-bye Heathcliff: Changing Heroes, Heroines, Roles and Values in Women's Category Romances*. New York: Greenwood Press, 1988.

Fromm, E. *The Art of Loving*. New York: Bantam, 1959.

Harlow, H. & Zimmerman, R. "Affectional Responses in the Infant Monkey." *Science*, 130 (1959): 421-432.

Hazen, C., & Shaver, P. "Romantic Love Conceptualized as an Attachment Process." *Journal of Personality and Social Psychology*, 52 (1987): 511-524.

Hendrick, C., & Hendrick, S. "A Theory and Method of Love." *Journal of Personality and Social Psychology*, 50 (1986): 392-402.

Kelley, H. H. "Love and Commitment." In H. H. Kelley, E. Berscheid, A. Christensen, J. H. Harvey, T. L. Huston, G. Levinger, E. McClintock, L. A. Peplau, & D. R. Peterson (eds.), *Close Relationships*. New York: Freeman, 1983.

Raskin, P. M. "The Relationship Between Identity and Intimacy in Early Adulthood," *Journal of Genetic Psychology*, 147 (1986): 167-181.

Walster, E., & Walster, G. W. *A New Look at Love*. Reading, MA: Addison-Wesley, 1978.

Questions

1. Create a list of words/concepts that are synonymous with or associated with the concept of love (e.g., appreciate, trust).

2. The essay distinguishes passionate love and companionate love. How can an understanding of this distinction help you develop loving relationships?

3. What connection is the author drawing between human love and divine love?

4. Considering the negative influence of popular culture (movies, music, soap operas) on the development of our concept of love, how do we discover the true nature of love as intended by God?

5. Pick a model of a loving relationship that you have seen grow and flourish. What are some of the strengths of this relationship that you have observed? Also pick a model of a loving relationship that degenerated. What are some of the weaknesses?

6. How does a better understanding/grasp of love lead us to a deeper faith in God?

8

Christel and Creation

Myriad treasures of wisdom and knowledge remain hidden within the physical world about us. Many of the weightier problems wrestled with since earliest history are intimately connected with the physical creation. These include predestination, providence, miracles, and such theories as that of evolution.

Patterns of The Physical
Here is a simple demonstration I want you to do. You will be fascinated with what happens. You will need two glasses of water and a soda straw (an eyedropper would be better, but that may not be as available as a straw). Fill one glass (or a bowl) with water and let it stand as you prepare the water in the second glass. Put about an inch of water in that glass, and add some coloring. If food coloring is not

available, you might try swishing a magic marker around in the water.

Now, dip the straw into the colored water and put your finger over the upper end, so that you can lift the straw and have a few drops of water inside it. Place the lower end of the straw about half an inch above the surface of the water in the full glass. Release your finger just enough to allow one drop to fall from the straw.

When the drop hits the surface, you should see a donut-shape ring form below the surface and go downward. If you vary the height from the straw to the surface or add some salt to either of the waters, you should see changes in the behavior of the shapes that form. Above a height of about an inch, rings no longer form, but instead a splash occurs and a small spike and droplet are formed.

What you saw was a *vortex ring*, a phenomenon associated with swirling motions, and quite common in air and water. Vortex rings are very complex and not understood in detail, but are an example of elements of the physical world about us that are a mystery. Yet, they do occur and always in the same way when conditions are identical.

This demonstration is an example of how easy it is to create unusual and unexpected results—and do it consistently—when conditions are proper for an unchanging pattern of the physical creation to apply.

As another example of possibly unexpected effects of nature's laws, consider the tides. Most people think they are caused by the gravitational pull of the moon on the waters of the earth. But, do you realize that the sun's contribution to tidal action is about half that of the moon's? And, it is the combination of these pulls that daily causes two unequal tidal patterns on the west coast of our country, two nearly identical tidal patterns on our east coast, and only one tide per day on a few coasts of the world! Also, even inland lakes have tides, but they are so small that they are masked by the normal wave action of the lakes.

The more one considers the physical creation, the more one realizes how little we know about its intricacy. Years ago I ran across an intriguing book, *Music of the Spheres*, by Guy Murchie, that has had an important influence on my thinking. Through a wide range of discussions of mysteries of the universe, Murchie offers insights into a world basically formed by wave motions, into the relationships of infinitesimal energy units of which everything is constituted, into the precise ratios of size, energy, and volume of physical objects (from bugs to elephants and trees), and into the apparent limits of both time and space, of which our current technologies are able to sample only a small portion experimentally.

A second book that increased my appreciation for the ultimate power and wisdom exhibited in the created world, *The Living Clocks*, by Ritchie R. Ward, describes the rhythms of life that exist in almost any aspect of the created that you can imagine: from the motion of charges in atomic structures—to the geologic cycles of the earth—to the cycles of the vastness of space and its bodies—to the motions of the oceans and the atmosphere—to the many interesting and varied patterns found in sea life—to the migratory and other curious cycles found in birds—to the daily and seasonal cycles that plants exhibit—to the myriad of different cycles that exist in the animal kingdom ranging from the amoeba to man. While the presence of so many different cycles is beyond comprehension, even more mind boggling is the fact that they all fit together to form a perfectly operating system.

In fact, the matter of cycles is of such rising interest that the Foundation for the Study of Cycles was founded in 1941 and has documented more that 3,000 cycles of all types. The executive director of the cycle foundation, Jeffrey

H. Horovitz, in the March 14, 1988, issue of *Insight* magazine, contends that "although the exact mechanisms relating sunspots and meteorologic cycles, lunar and geologic cycles, climate and crop, flora and fauna cycles are not fully understood, the coincidences of similar cycles are too pervasive to be explained by mere chance." To those of faith in the Creator, the conclusion of Horovitz is certainly nothing new, although confirming.

Christ's Role in the Creation

We all know that the Bible begins with the statement that in the beginning God created the heavens and the earth, and that the creation is described as having been completed in six days. But, where does Christ enter in? The words of Hebrews 1:2 teach that, first, God appointed Christ heir of all things and, secondly, through Christ God made the universe. And, verse 10 tells us that Christ laid the foundations of the earth, and that the heavens are the work of Christ's hands. Verses 11 and 12 reveal that the creation will perish, with Christ rolling them up like a garment.

The first three verses of the gospel of John expand upon these relationships: the Word, which we understand to be Christ, was in the beginning, was with God, and was God. Further, we specifically find, "Through him (Christ) all things were made; without him nothing was made that has been made." Our physical world was made *through* and *by* Christ.

In the words of Colossians 1:15-17, the influence and supremacy of Christ is expanded beyond the physical. There we have an impressive list of characteristics of Christ that pertain to the physical world:

1. He is the image of the invisible God
2. He is the firstborn of all creation
3. By him all things were created

4. All things were created by him and for him
5. He is before all things
6. In him all things hold together.

Particularly note the centrality of the fourth item of the list above. The passage further describes the created things in heaven, of earth, visible, and invisible, including thrones and powers and rulers and authorities, all of which are non-physical but which exist within our physical environment. The ultimate truth, and the one we probably understand least, is that all things are said to be created *for* Christ!

The Theories of Science

Knowledge about our physical world is increasing at an exponential rate, and fortunately much of it has found application for the benefit of mankind. However, nearly all new knowledge raises as many questions as it answers, if not more.

For example, the theory of natural selection, commonly known as the theory of evolution, was a product of Charles Darwin's effort to understand the world. In 1835, he visited the Galapogos islands where he found an amazing array of animals, many bizarre in feature, that are not found elsewhere on earth. Using scientific methods for collecting and interpreting data, Darwin theorized how the physical world and its occupants were formed—a theory based on what he observed in the Galapogos, pieced together and extrapolated to include *all* living creation. That very strained and highly unsupported extrapolation has unfortunately been widely accepted by those without faith in God.

The theory of evolution has been promoted as truth rather than just theory. Incidentally, the order of creation found in Darwin's theory is very similar to the Genesis account of creation, which moves from the origin of the heavens and the earth to separation of the waters to vegetation to the heavenly lights to birds and water creatures to animals and finally to man. The answers to the innumerable questions about details of the creation indeed remain unknown, no doubt as part of the treasures of wisdom and knowledge hidden in Christ.

One concept of evolution *is* familiar to all: many things do change and develop new attributes. New varieties of plants are commonplace, as are new breeds of animals, and even new strains of viruses. The average heights of Americans are evolving, as well as our cultural patterns and attitudes. Individually, over our lifetime we evolve physically, attitudinally, and emotionally. Evolution, in this sense, is a normal part of life. It is even evident in the relationship of God and man, for that relationship moved from one of man's perfection upon creation to his fall, and then through the Patriarchal and Mosaic ages to the Christian age and the return of man to God's favor. Even our personal relationships with God evolve over our lifetime as we learn and experience.

While Darwin's conclusions were based upon limited data and much speculation, pure scientific methods have produced a vast number of theories, many supported by mathematical formulations, that have led to important advances in technology and the comfort and quality of life. Theories based on well researched quantitative data have been the foundation of air travel, our efforts in space travel and exploration, electronics of all kinds, long distance communication, medical advances, and other familiar aspects of our life.

While many theories, or formulas if you please, have been considered sound and have been the basis of many successful applications, research at times yields results that call established formulas into question. For example, only recently researchers have released data that refute the exactness of Newton's law of gravity, which may be the most widely known and trusted theory ever formulated. The new information, even if found reliable after extended investigation, will not affect our use of the familiar form of the law except in those special applications that require great precision of calculation. Newton's law and other cases, sprinkled throughout the history of scientific investigation, vividly illustrate that mankind's knowledge of that which is about us is far less than what is to be known about it. Much is still hidden.

A Perspective on Scientific Discoveries

As science progresses, the limits of knowledge expand inexorably inward toward smaller and smaller details, as well as outward toward vastness that seems to be limitless. As amazing as the discoveries are, one must keep in mind one fact that is seldom mentioned—the features and processes that research brings to our understanding have always been part of the creation; they are not just now evolving. The details and intricacies that are yet hidden from our understanding are, no doubt, part of the hidden wisdom and knowledge to which our theme passage alludes. Are we so naive as to believe they came into existence only recently and were observed? Is the law of gravity evolving? Are the laws of cooling bodies different from those when the earth was formed? Has not water always been water as we know it today? Has its freezing point changed? I would find it hard to believe!

As one of many possible examples, consider the phenomenon known as superconductivity, which was first observed and reported in 1911. All materials offer resistance to the flow of electricity through them, some more than others. However, in 1911 some materials were found to suddenly lose *all* resistance to electrical flow when they are subjected to very cold temperatures, temperatures close to absolute zero.

Although this characteristic was known, the costs of obtaining the low temperatures needed kept that knowledge from having practical use until 1973 when new materials, quite by accident, were found to superconduct at higher temperatures. Since 1986 there has been a vigorous race involving Japanese, US, and Swiss scientists to find materials that will possess superconducting properties at room temperatures. If and when that happens, the world may be influenced fully as much as it was by the introduction of electricity or the computer.

The point here is not to describe a fantastic frontier of science, but rather to emphasize that superconductivity was one of the hidden treasures of the original creation that is only now being revealed. There is no reason to doubt that Adam and Eve could have developed and used superconducting materials if they had had the proper equipment and knowledge to do so. The reason they did not was certainly not that the phenomenon of superconductivity did not exist in the same materials in which it was found in 1911.

Superconductivity is but one of a host of things that were hidden in the treasures of wisdom and knowledge during creation, but one which is now being revealed. Without doubt the succession of amazing revelations of hidden treasures will continue as long as the world stands. Moreover, if the trend indicated by the history of technology and science continues, these "discoveries" will be proclaimed at an increasing rate.

One ironic part of the succession of scientific advances is that, to some people, these advances confirm the wisdom and evolution of the human to higher and higher planes. To others, the new knowledge and its applications are additional reinforcement of a basic belief in God's existence, power, and ever presence.

God and Creation

While we know relatively little of God's will and purposes in relation to the physical creation, and while there are relationships between Christ, God, and creation that are not fully clear, there are some very important insights revealed by the scriptures. For instance, we know that the creator was pleased with what he created, for the description of the creation in Genesis ends with the statement that God saw that all he made was good.

Not only was God pleased with what he created, but he also remains the preserver and provider for all creation. In Psalms 46, David proclaimed, "God is our refuge and strength, an ever-present help in trouble. Therefore we will not fear ."

What determines the destiny of God's creation? Are we puppets in the hand of God? In Jeremiah 27:5-6, God warned rulers who were opposing Israel that with power he made the earth, the people, and the animals—and adds that he will give it to anyone he pleases! Creation is at the pleasure of God, and will be controlled by him. The comforting aspect of God's control is that he has promised to be the refuge, guide, and provider for those who are his. What could be more comforting than a firm conviction that indeed, as Romans 8:28 promises, all things will work together for good to those who love the Lord?

We are familiar with God's providential oversight of the patriarchs, and of the many wonders performed during the journey of the children of Israel from Egypt to the promised land. The hand of the creator caused earthquakes, hail, rains, droughts, famines, hordes of noxious animals or insects, and numerous other demonstrations of nature in dealing with those who opposed the Lord. Conversely, that same hand provided manna, produced water, withheld rivers, provided ways for escaping dangers, and in many other ways used creation to provide for and sustain believers.

Beyond exercising control of the physical world to resist the wicked and provide for the faithful, God has also exhibited his control over the universe for another purpose—the creation of faith in the power and sovereignty of the Lord. Such control is seen from the plagues of Egypt to the healing and other miracles performed by Christ and the apostles. Jonah certainly was made aware of God's control of nature through the fish God prepared to swallow Jonah in his disobedience, and later through the vine and worm that God prepared to instruct Jonah.

God's Plan of Revelation

It is not strange that God has chosen to reveal the mysteries of the physical in a continuing succession that man can understand and apply. After all, that is exactly what he did in revealing, from the time of the patriarchs through that of the apostles, the spiritual blessings concerning Christ and redemption. As spiritual mysteries and blessings were planned and hidden until the appropriate time, so have the many mysteries and blessings of the physical creation been reserved until the time of God's choosing.

And so, even though I have come to know and understand many of the things that mankind has learned of the physical world, I know that there are many more things that I do not know—nor does any other person know them. Though I see the mountains and the seas and the skies, I know that there are within them atom worlds that have within them other atom worlds, and that within the seas there are other seas, and that beyond the skies there are other skies and stars and even universes. Indeed, I continually seek for a better understanding of the mysteries and hidden things within the things I see and feel and touch, knowing they are there and speak of both God and Christ. Will you not join me in making the words of Psalms 104: 24 part of our principal understandings of life: "O Lord, how manifold are thy works! In wisdom hast thou made them all: the earth is full of thy riches."

Hugh F. Keedy, Ph.D.
Professor Emeritus of Engineering Science
Vanderbilt University

Questions

1.   What evidence of order, cycles, rhythms, do you observe in nature? What conclusions do you draw from this evidence?

2.   What relationship do you see between scientific advances and faith? For some people, the succession of scientific advances "confirms the wisdom and evolution of the human to higher and higher planes." For others it reinforces a basic belief in God's existence. Explain why.

3.   To you, what is the most amazing scientific discovery you have learned about? What makes it amazing to you?

4.   How do you see nature and history being used by God today to create faith?

5.   In your own words, what is the basis of your faith in God?
      a.   If someone asked you why you believe in God, what would you answer?
      b.   Write an essay in which you explain why you believe in God.

9

What I Learned in School

Mr. Christian was the best teacher I have ever known, and I've known a few. This teacher, though, taught me more about learning, about students, about teaching with passion, about joys and not-so-joys than all my years of schooling activities combined. And there have been a few years, too.

I have been a part of schools and education since playing at the ages of two and three in the back of my grandmother's schoolroom. It was great fun to have free reign of the books and papers. Crayons were magic wands, and books were magic carpets. I remember the music most of all; that's only logical, because two-year-olds remember music before language.

I remember the music, too, of first grade, when the class stood and sang "Good Morning to You" upon the arrival of our teacher. There were various chants and melodies through elementary and high school, all leading me to be a teacher. I don't remember ever having cognitively made the decision. I just don't remember ever having cognitively decided on anything else. So, it was done.

I watched my university professors and learned under my mentors the ways of instruction in the classroom. They were learned men and women, outstanding educators and role models. To this day, I regard them as among the elite in classroom effectiveness, but Mr. Christian was the best.

He was the sixth grade teacher on a campus that housed grades one through six. That position made him the "King of the Mountain" teacher, as students rightfully claimed their thrones of leadership over the younger ones on campus.

By the sixth grade, and even much earlier, many of the potential problems of secondary student years were already visible and damaging. Following some student careers into years beyond the elementary campus provided little surprise for the veteran elementary faculty. So, sixth grade, by design and by function, was a tough year for any teacher.

And especially, it seemed to be so for one particular class of students, that sixth grade class where I just happened to be placed by birth and not by choice. The campus leadership had carefully placed several of the upcoming "Mountain Kings" during second, third, and on grades to keep them separated. Counselors were just about out of configurations to keep volatile students placed apart.

So it seemed an incredible shock to administration, faculty, parents, and students alike when Mr. Christian filed his special request for class roster in the upcoming school year. Knowing these kids as well as anyone did (and they were notorious), Mr. Christian was specifically asking, by request yet, for the worst kids in school, and certainly the worst combination of personalities. And much to my twelve-year-old chagrin, I was on the list, as ballast, I suppose.

What a year! I spent most of the time trying to figure out what he was trying to accomplish with this bunch of renegades. Losers, all. Of course, with this group, I felt very much the observer and not the participant, so I am excluding myself with these descriptive terms. But for everyone else, losers, all.

Mr. Christian, himself, made little sense to me, either. Any other teacher would have avoided this group, and when faced with the inevitable, would have delivered the law with great grimace and ceremony.

He requested them, though. Puzzlement enough then, and sometimes even now, after college degrees and years in the classroom. Knowing now what I did not know then, I'm still not sure I could do what he did.

The first day of school, I planned for riot police and mayhem. He simply called each one of the unpleasants by name and issued a personal invitation to join him in the sixth grade. I was amazed. (I spent much of the year amazed.) Although seldom at a loss for words or negative behaviors, each one instead simply took a place in the room. We were to instruction in a matter of minutes.

I expected the instruction to be typical school: books about stuff I already knew or books about stuff I didn't understand, but mostly books and worksheets and notebooks and tests and grades and homework and make-up grades and schooling agendas. An academic calendar would occasionally adjust to school plays or other such departures, but each day was largely like the last . . . and the next.

Thus, when Mr. Christian started explaining new material using ordinary kid-stuff, I was delighted. In fact, I didn't even know I was learning anything, because we were talking about my everyday world: sports and scouting and growing up and dreaming and thinking about the future. This was my world. Even the hard-core trouble-makers learned.

Some of them became the classic prototype who confronted me in later years when I entered the classroom as a teacher. Though names and cultural customs changed, the personalities and behaviors were the same. And while I was confused at the way Mr. Christian handled the beasties during my sixth grade year, I have since seen the wisdom of his methods.

He had a different approach for each student. He could not have read the recent research about individual learning styles or left-brain right-brain learning theories. The literature, of course, has been published in the several years between my sixth grade year and now, but it was not available then. At reading the cutting-edge of pedagogical thinking today, I quickly go back to that classroom to see it in practice, thirty years before press.

Pete was the most remarkable of this ragtag class. He learned with his mouth. Mr. Christian could hardly finish a sentence before Pete would jump in, make some premature conclusive statement, then close the whole matter with his authoritative style. Too bad he didn't know what he was talking about most of the time. He was as apt to respond with his fists, too, to add conviction and commitment to his point. Again, he was usually wrong.

As I have encountered various Petes along my career, my natural inclination has been to force them to be quiet and be still, with relative degrees of success. I have since learned that if the Pete-type learners are not talking, they're not learning either. I have also learned to appreciate passion in a student, even when he or she is wrong. At least the noisy one is thinking!

Mr. Christian identified quickly the inherent leadership ability in Pete, though it took me a long time to see it. Rather than quiet the motor-mouth, Mr. Christian captured Pete's demand to know and to understand. Through as much repetition as the situation required, Mr. Christian finally talked Pete around to seeing the point, and usually without bloodshed. This teacher remained calm during every blurt-out and/or shoot-out, repaired the damage, and stayed with the instruction until even Pete figured it out.

Then there were the twins, Johnnie and Jamie. These were tough boys, language, clothing, mannerisms, and behaviors consistent with their home environment. I often sensed that they were in competition, not only with themselves, but with their father, for tough-guy title. Their dad drove a tractor-trailer rig with lightning bolts painted on the cab. It fit.

The unwritten rule was that you avoided these two. Mr. Christian hadn't heard the rule. He gave these guys the same invitations to learn that he gave everyone else. He gave them individual dignity, not always a given with twins, and perspective on the future. These boys were offered a different role model than their father. Above all, he gave them the freedom to make choices about their lives.

Maggie was also in this group, Maggie, a twelve-year-old future . . . well, sixth graders weren't supposed to know those words, but we all knew enough about Maggie already. I couldn't believe that Mr. Christian would talk to her at all, knowing her reputation, much less ask her to be in the class. Professionally, that move could be highly dangerous for him.

He tolerated absolutely no ridicule of Maggie. He treated her with kindness and respect and demanded that we do the same. She began to feel worthy, and we forgot about all the stories. Her leadership skills began to emerge, so that soon, she was leading the group, often first in line and often with the first comments.

The fact that he would encourage leadership skills in girls, especially this one, gave us reason to examine our own talents and abilities in light of what we could accomplish, rather than what critics would tell us we could accomplish. I wonder how many from that class have taken one more step with courage because Mr. Christian would not let us destroy Maggie. I would imagine all of us.

Matt had money, so we hated him. I don't know why that always went together, but Matt's money was his biggest enemy. I think Matt would have gladly thrown it all away for one good friend. Mr. Christian helped all of us get around that barrier, so that we could become friends with Matt. He taught us the value of money, which isn't much; he taught us the value of loving each other, which is everything. Matt, money and all, became a lifetime friend.

Lucas kept wanting to fix sick animals. He had a compassion for creatures in pain and wanted to help them. That was in direct opposition to any sixth grader's natural inclination to pull various wings and legs off insects. So, of course, we gave him all kinds of trouble. Rather than isolate Lucas from all the rest of us, Mr. Christian taught us how to help hurting animals, how to bandage injuries so they could heal and how to take the fright away from a scared kitten. I don't know that any of us could spell compassion in the sixth grade, but we were learning what it meant.

Jud was a thief. Everybody knew it, so of course, none of us trusted him with anything. That was simply the rule, and it made sense to all of us. What didn't make sense was when Mr. Christian made Jud class treasurer. My first assumption was that Mr. Christian didn't know about Jud, and that as soon as he did, he would take the class money and give it to a more responsible student. It never happened. Mr. Christian just kept on investing faith in Jud, hoping that one day Jud would accept the gifts of repeated opportunity. Sadly, that too never happened.

Realizing that I cannot dictate my students' reactions to my invitations to learn has been and still is a difficult lesson for me. I have lost my share, despite my every effort. Every teacher has to deal with this. In the constant frustration of trying to reach one who will not be reached, I have tried and failed to force learning, force consensus, demand obedience, save my own face. Then, as often as not, I give up. None of that works, of course. I learned two things from watching Mr. Christian and Jud: the student will make decisions that relate to his or her life, and I can never, never, never give up. These two lessons have carried me through many a rough situation.

There would be the teacher's pet. In this case, though, none of us felt isolated or violated. Mr. Christian loved all of us, and we knew it, so the fact that he loved one of us deeply didn't seem to be much of a problem. We were each accepted on our own merits, as individuals, each with tasks and unique gifts to complete those tasks.

While that didn't particularly bother anyone, Tommy did. He drove everybody crazy. Somebody must have teased him about the tooth-fairy or Santa Claus, because Tommy wouldn't believe anything unless he could see it. Everything had to be proven; he had to add up all the numbers in the multiplication tables before he would believe that 7 X 8 is 56 or 9 X 9 is 81. He had to conduct all the experiments himself and hold all the baby animals himself before he would believe anything. What a nuisance! Mr. Christian had to teach everything at least three times: once for Pete, who was running ahead of everybody, once for the normal ones, and once especially for Tommy, who always said, "I don't believe it."

That's a tough situation for a teacher, too. After your best presentation (with "visuals" yet), some mouthy one, who probably wasn't paying attention in the first place, whines, "I don't understand." Referring said child to the text usually doesn't help much. nor does embarrassing the student or harping for not paying attention. Mr. Christian simply taught it again, and again, and again, until Tommy had enough evidence to be satisfied.

As if one weren't enough, there was another set of siblings, and this before much of the recent studies on birth order and first child giftedness. These two girls weren't twins, but they were sisters. Marty and Mary were their names. Mary had been held back a year because she couldn't attend to task, just couldn't get her work finished. Marty, of course, completed all her work first. It was perfect. We hated her.

Mary was introspective and quiet, mostly. We all just assumed that she was lazy or incapable. Sixth graders had all kinds of names for people like that. We were vicious; even Marty turned on her at times. Mr. Christian shocked us all one day, during one of our self-righteous academic tirades, by instructing us to leave Mary alone. He defended her and even praised her for her behavior.

But that wasn't even the biggest surprise with these two girls. That happened one day during the spring. Their little brother Larry was playing baseball with his second grade class. As it would happen, the kid got clobbered in the head with a baseball bat. It was very serious on the playground that day. As it turned out, Larry was eventually going to be fine, but the atmosphere was thick for a while. I simply could not understand Mr. Christian's reaction to the episode.

The two girls were crying and so were most of the other kids. I don't know what I expected Mr. Christian to do, but I didn't expect this: he started crying, too. Now first of all, teachers just didn't do this, especially male teachers. It just never occurred to any of us that teachers were human, just like we were. The assumption was that Mr. Christian was born at the age of thirty and had been thirty for several years. We did not realize that he had feelings and heartache and emotions and disappointments, just like us. I guess we assumed that teachers were somewhat like alarm clocks that wind up and down until a bell goes off.

Most of us stopped crying and just stared at him. He was human. When we hurt, he hurt. When we cried, he cried. He felt so deeply for us that our hearts became his.

I learned that day what teaching is all about: a teacher's heart becomes one with the student. Then, the teacher can teach, and the student can learn. Any success I have experienced in the classroom as a teacher stems from that relationship. Any failure I have shared has been in violation of that relationship.

It would be reasonable to assume that the year was dedicated to riot-control. With the combination of opposing personalities and typical sixth-grade aversion to anything resembling rational thought, were the nine months spent without significant bloodletting, the year would have been a success. But we actually learned. The beauty of learning is that we are all still learning as our years of living finally show us the truths that Mr. Christian gave us, if only in rote packages until we would internalize their meaning.

I'll never forget the close of school. Going to the junior high for seventh grade was terrifying enough, but going without Mr. Christian held no interest for me whatsoever. None of us wanted to leave. At the beginning of the year, we could hardly stand the sight of each other and unilaterally refused to learn anything. At the end, we shared a love and hunger for understanding that still burns. He gave us gifts of confidence with humility and ration with thinking. He gave us a model of leadership that would serve people rather than rule them. He gave us a value system that ignores artificial definitions and relies on lasting ones.

How did he do this? How did he select the worst raggle of brats and turn them into servant leaders? How did he pick the slowest learners and the loudest talkers and turn them into academic giants? How did he give us the confidence to continue on our own, when we face a world horribly akin to our sixth grade class?

One hundred years of research have brought the teaching profession significant truths about classroom instruction, which include learning styles, cognitive mapping, motivational strategies, thinking patterns, bonding, reinforcement, coding, grouping and on and on. Mr. Christian gave the same truths to an undeserving lot in a single sixth grade year. Simply:

- every student deserves individual recognition and dignity;
- every student can develop if given the right opportunity;
- learning is continual and constant, with applications varying throughout a lifetime;
- every student is "home-schooled" to some extent, either for good or bad;
- students learn in different ways;
- the role of a teacher is the role of a servant-leader;
- that we seek and love the Creator of an ordered cosmos;
- that we love each other.

The more my teaching resembles that of Mr. Christian, the more my students celebrate who they are and share their gifts with each other. They are hungry to learn. They teach each other, and they teach me.

Anytime that is not happening in my classroom, I look for the path that leads away from Mr. Christian's teaching style. Every time, I have ventured into power leadership rather than servant leadership, or meeting my own needs rather than my students'. It never fails that learning falls apart at this point.

It follows, too, that learning resumes when I serve my students as I would the children of God. Learning resumes when I serve their needs to grow rather than my needs to hold some artificial power. Learning resumes when I feel their hearts rather than close mine to them. Learning thrives when I recognize the hand of the Creator in each of them and the value that their lives hold in Heaven. I can hardly keep up with their demands to know when I acknowledge the gifts that they hold and the dreams that they dream.

My life was changed by this sixth grade teacher. My prayer is that you had a teacher like Mr. Christian, a teacher who gave your life meaning, purpose, and direction. And as you consider those teachers you had in your earlier years, you might recognize this one easily by his first name—Jesus.

To think he selected me to be one of His!

Jeri Pfeifer, Ed.D.
Associate Professor of Education
Assistant Vice-President for Enrollment
Management
Abilene Christian University

Questions

1. How did Mr. Christian give the students "individual dignity"?

2. Briefly describe some significant truth you have learned from a master teacher and relate the situation/s that helped you learn that truth.

3. What analogy do you see between the students in the essay and Biblical characters?

4. Think of a teacher you have had who exemplifies Jesus' master teaching. Refer to the specific truths listed in the conclusion of the essay. Choose at least three and describe the situation for each one that illustrates how the teacher practiced the principle or method you chose from the list. Think of situations in which you have seen teachers practice or prove these truths.

10

Strategic Initiative

Every church leader at some time has grappled with the question: Where should the Church be headed? It's a simple and straightforward question. Yet many church leaders are puzzled, perplexed, and deeply troubled by this question, and with good reason. The question cuts to the nature and purpose of the Church and to the leaders' vision of what the Church should become. It is a challenging question about congregational *strategy*. It assumes that no matter how strong a congregation's present position, the status quo is always on trial.

An increasing number of corporations and institutions are using strategic management concepts and techniques to make effective decisions. Unfortunately, few church leaders seem to consider the strategy concept until their congregations face formidable problems. Yet they claim to follow one of the greatest strategists of all time—

Jesus Christ. Growing churches are very provocative, goal-oriented, and evangelistic. Their leaders seize the moment. They take strategic initiative and move forward to the glory of God. Let's define and illustrate what's involved.

Strategic Initiative and the Church

Strategy is derived from the Greek word *strategos* and refers to a military general. Originally a term applied to warfare and the exercise of large military movements and operations of war, *strategy* may seem a strange word to link with the Church. However, on an earthly plane, some churches resemble battlefields. Members argue, fight, and sue one another. One congregation defames another congregation. On a heavenly plane, we are at war against "the rulers, the authorities, the powers of darkness, and the spiritual forces of evil" (Ephesians 6:12).

These earthly and heavenly wars raise an interesting question: Who are we fighting against? Is it Satan? The "World"? Ourselves? Other churches? Corporate America? Hugh Hefner? It is doubtful that Satan distinguishes between the heavenly and earthly planes; they are one and the same to him. He seems to move freely between the physical, real world (e.g., Job) and the spiritual world (e.g., the temptation of Jesus). In such an uncertain world and with such a mobile enemy, strategy is a must.

Initiative refers to the determination to take the first step toward a goal or goals (i.e., the basic purpose of the Church) and then to keep moving toward it. The *American Heritage Dictionary* (Second College Edition) defines initiative as "the power, ability, or instinct to begin or follow through energetically with a plan or task." The apostle Paul might have described it in these terms—pressing on and living up to what we have attained (Philippians 3:12,16). In all of Paul's work we see this basically dual objective: (1) never being satisfied with where he is now (spiritually), and

(2) pressing on (using his God-given initiative). Similarly, the Church can not be content with its unfinished work.

Initiative is a highly prized trait in managers and employees. In order for our churches to avoid stagnation, decline, and death, they also must use a rational approach toward anticipating, responding to, and altering the future. They must exert a strategic initiative. God has always used strategists with initiative to accomplish His will (e.g., Joseph, Gideon, David, Nehemiah, Paul). Today is no different.

Strategic Initiative and Leadership

To understand strategic initiative and how it relates to church leadership, we must consider two critical facets: *what* the congregation wants to be and *how* it should get there. While both are integral to long-range thinking, they must not be confused. The Church's future self-definition—what it wants to be—and its planning and operational decision making—how it gets there—are related by separate dimensions. Since what a congregation wants to be sets direction, it must be formulated prior to long-range planning and the day-to-day decision making that follows.

The Church is a living organism; it must adapt to survive. Some congregations adapt by focusing primarily on present operations. They continually try to improve operating efficiency. However, if a congregation is headed in the wrong direction, the last thing it needs is to get there more efficiently. And even if a congregation is headed in the right direction, it surely does not need to have that direction unwittingly changed by operational action taken in a strategic void.

Other congregations adapt for survival via a well-defined strategy. They do not assume current operations as a given for the future but ask: What's happening in the world around us? What does that suggest about our current direction? They know that to survive in an environment of turbulent change, operational planning must proceed within the framework of their strategy.

What is Strategic Leadership?

Every congregation has a momentum or direction. It is headed somewhere. Leaders who do not consciously set strategy risk having their direction developed implicitly, haphazardly, or by others. Strategic leadership is generally defined, therefore, as the formulation, implementation, and evaluation of actions that enable an organization to achieve its objectives.

Strategy assumes church leaders will continually monitor key internal and external events and trends, that they will pursue strategies that capitalize on internal strengths, take advantage of external opportunities, mitigate internal weaknesses, and avoid or mollify the impact of external threats. We need environmental scanners and market analysts within the Church. We need leaders who keep up with the megatrends (i.e., changes) our world is encountering. These processes are the essence of strategic leadership! To survive today's spiritual competition, leaders must identify the need for and adapt to changes. This requires research, analysis, decision making, commitment, and discipline. The best-formulated strategies in the world are no good if they cannot be implemented successfully.

The Need for Strategy

In business, "strategic management" was first used during the 1950s and 1960s when new markets were emerging and expanding. Then during the early 1970s growth began stagnating, and in the mid-1980s production was declining. Strategy thus became a central concept for managing organizational resources to achieve long-range objectives. It was assumed that the fundamental strength of a company could be related to certain strategic process potentials (e.g., competitiveness, flexibility, implementability, etc.).

In both business and the Church, the need for strategy is based on three other important needs. According to Tregoe and Zimmerman, these include:

1. *the need for focus*—many statements of strategy are just too abstract to provide guidance to key decision makers;
2. *the need for congruence*—there is a lack of a common way to tie together needed directions;
3. *the need to respond strategically to change.* (28-29)

When you listen to what church leaders are saying, when you examine their statements of strategy, you come away knowing that often their congregations' strategies are vague, or that they lack specificity, or that they are too massive and complicated to serve as a framework to guide key decision makers. For a congregation to really "pull together" strategically, there must be congruence between the strategy set by the leaders and the strategies set by others in the congregation.

A Chinese proverb says, "Every change brings an opportunity." It also can bring a threat. All congregations face change. How well the Church negotiates the hurdles of change is key to its survival and success. Some change is external. It occurs "outside" the congregation—in the environment—and is beyond a congregation's immediate control. Other change is internal. It occurs "inside" a congregation and is directly within its sphere of decision-making capability. In spite of the differences between external and internal change, there is one important similarity: both require raising strategic questions first, before any action is taken.

The Search for Initiative

The whole notion of strategic initiative and leadership may present a dilemma. That is, whom do we select as leaders or strategists to either keep the Church headed in the right direction or to turn it around if it is struggling or failing. Insight about the types of people Jesus called to his ministry can be found in Luke 5:1-11. These individuals were (1) willing to work, (2) obedient to His commands, (3) honest in assessing themselves, and (4) willing to make sacrifices (Ash 99). In essence, they were a group willing to exercise their initiative.

Willing to Work

Jesus picked men who worked with their hands (Luke 5:2b, 5a). Peter, Andrew, James, and John may be the principals in this story (Mark 1:16-21). These men did not fish for fun; this was not a weekend fishing/camping expedition. This was a job which gave them only the afternoons to themselves. Night, apparently, was the best fishing time; the worst time was the morning when the sun was glistening on the water. So they would fish all night and then spend a good part of the morning cleaning their nets. That's what they were doing when Jesus arrived on the scene and starting issuing instructions to them. Yet, after working all night and most of the morning, they were willing to go out onto the water again simply because Jesus asked them to. It had been a fruitless night; they were tired, and Jesus had just made them sit through a sermon; but, because He said so they worked a little longer.

The lack of work was what got one church into trouble (2 Thessalonians 3:6-13). Many had quit their jobs (i.e., work) because they thought the Lord would come soon. The result of their lack of work was *busibodiness*. (Sometimes it is the ones who work the most who talk the least and vice-versa). Paul exhorted them (and us) to work in quietness; to earn their own living, not to be a burden on others; and to not grow tired of working. Jesus picked people who were very used to work and who were not afraid of it.

Obedient

Peter and the others obeyed seemingly without reservation (Luke 5:5b). They may not have completely understood why the Lord was commanding certain things, but they obeyed anyway. Sometimes we don't understand either. Remember Ananias being told to baptize Saul, or Peter being told to eat of the animals that God showed to him in the dream. The story of Abraham being told to sacrifice his son is a prime example. They didn't understand, but they obeyed.

Obedience is hard in a land of individuality like ours. It is an acknowledgment that someone besides us knows what's best for us. Our families are testimony to the struggle between individuality and obedience, between freedom and anarchy. Parents are holding on to their teenagers, hoping against hope to keep them from being too contaminated by the world, and the teens are struggling with every fiber to release themselves from parental grip in order to live their own lives. At some point parents release, with the promise that as God provided for Abraham, He will also provide for their children, or with the knowledge that if someone doesn't release they'll kill each other. But obedience is hard; giving up self-control is hard, even to one who loves us.

Honest in Assessing Themselves

Peter came to the realization that he was a sinner. In fact, he was so painfully aware of his depravity that he fell to his knees in a boat full of slithering fish. The incredible thing about Peter throughout the New Testament (and David in the Old Testament) is his self-assessing powers. He stumbles so often and yet realizes that he has limitations: the denial, the walk on water, the time he was rebuked by Paul for his hypocrisy among the Gentiles. We also live with certain limitations.

This incident (v. 8) raises a question: How often do we assess ourselves? Judging others is so much easier than looking inside ourselves. We may judge others to avoid judging ourselves. Yet Jesus demands that His followers constantly evaluate themselves: "Take heed, lest ye fall." When we realize that we are sinners in need of a saviour, we have made the first step toward growth. Honest self-assessment—it's hard work.

Willing to Make Sacrifices

There was no free ride for these early followers. They left everything to follow Jesus: their catch, their boats, jobs, means of livelihood, homes, and so on. Their lives began to revolve around a new center. The discipline once devoted to fishing now was devoted to spiritual ends. There is a remarkable trust here, and it is based on the assumption that Jesus could supply any needs just as he had supplied the fish.

Would-be followers in Luke 9:57-62 were asked to count the cost and follow Jesus, but refused. The answer to that call to sacrifice in order to follow has not changed: "No one who puts his hand to the plow and looks back is fit for the Kingdom of God."

The cost of following is high. It involves giving up and giving of self. Listen to these words of one of God's greatest followers:

"For to me, to live is Christ and to die is gain."

"Each of you should look not only to your own interests, but also to the interests of others."

"Continue to work out your salvation with fear and trembling, for it is God who works in you to will and to act according to his good purpose."

"I know what it is to be in need, and I know what it is to have plenty. I have learned the secret of being content in any and every situation, whether well fed or hungry, whether living in plenty or in want. I can do everything through him who gives me strength."

All these statements were written to the Philippian church while Paul was in prison for following Jesus. What is our willing-to-make-sacrifices quotient? Sacrificial living—it's hard work.

Initiators

When one inquires as to why Jesus selected the followers He did, the answer partially lies in the fact that he recognized in them a willingness to exercise their initiative. Sending out the Twelve on a trial-run missionary campaign, He told them:

I am sending you out like sheep among wolves.
Therefore be as shrewd as snakes and as innocent as doves. But be on your guard against men; they will hand you over to the local councils and flog you in their

synagogues. On my account you will be
brought before governors and kings as
witnesses to them and to the Gentiles.
(Matthew 10:16-18)

Jesus knew his apostles were capable of being "as
shrewd as snakes and as innocent as doves." He knew they
were capable of using their own initiative to perform His
work. But He also knew that before He could develop their
initiative, He would have to give them the initiative. He
then allowed them to act on their own and then to report
back to Him what happened. The result:

> "They went out and preached that people
> should repent.
> They drove out many demons and anointed
> many sick people with oil and healed them."
> (Mark 6:12-13)

On another occasion Jesus sent seventy-two others to
proclaim the good tidings of the kingdom. He transferred
initiative to them, and they returned from their missionary
campaign with joy, proclaiming, "Lord, even the demons
submit to us in your name." Jesus replied, "I saw Satan fall
like lightning from heaven . . . . rejoice that your names are
written in heaven" (Luke 10:17-20). The leader's job, so
amply demonstrated by our Lord, is to give followers no
choice but to choose and master their own initiative.

Oncken and Wass, in their classic article on time
management, say there are five degrees of initiative a leader
can exercise:

1. *wait* until told (lowest initiative);
2. *ask* what to do;
3. *recommend*, then take resulting action;

4. *act*, but advise at once; and
5. *act* on own, then routinely report (highest initiative). (79)

Two of the gravest problems in the Church today center around people not using their God-given initiative and leaders stifling people from using this initiative.

Conclusion

What the Church needs today (and what it has probably always needed) is change in the way it does things. It needs new models of vision, communication, and motivation. It needs to restore its competitiveness with the outside world. The Church needs to actively compete for leaders, souls, members, funds, and so on. But most of all, it needs a new strategic initiative. This need must be met before the Church loses this generation, plus the oncoming generation. Our leaders must stop their practices of being so worried about doing wrong that they can't do what's right. They must exercise their initiative just as the people Jesus chose did.

This change in our leaders will also include a change in vision, strategy, communication, and motivation. A new *vision* for the Lord's work is necessary because without a vision God's people perish (Proverbs 29:18). A new emphasis on *strategy* is important because our struggle is not against flesh and blood (Ephesians 6:12). A new emphasis on *communication* is needed because dreams must be put into words (Joel 2:28-29; Romans 10:13-18). New styles of *motivation* are needed because there are still people to be saved (Matthew 28:19-20) and churches to be grown (Acts 2:14-47).

The incorporation of a new synergistic combination of initiative, leadership, vision, strategy, communication, and motivation necessitates new expectations of our present leaders. They must not only adopt the leadership pattern of Jesus, but they must also use their congregations' strengths to (1) compensate for any weaknesses, (2) ward off possible threats, and (3) take advantage of emerging opportunities. They must be open to change, encourage change, and control the dynamics of change. They must take the strategic initiative and respond to a changing membership.

Phillip V. Lewis, Ed.D
Duniven Distinguished Professor of
Management
Abilene Christian University

William J. Mitchell
MPA student, Texas A&M University

WORKS CITED

Ash, A. L. *Commentary on Luke.* Abilene, Texas: ACU Press, 1972.

Oncken, Jr. & Wass, D. L. "Management Time: Who's Got the Monkey?" *Harvard Business* Review 52 (1974): 75-80.

Tregoe, B. B. & Zimmerman, J. W. *Top Management Strategy.* New York: Simon and Schuster, 1980.

Questions

1. In a teacher/student relationship, who exercises the initiative, the teacher or the student? Explain your perspective, keeping in mind the connotation of "initiative" in the essay.

2. What changes in church leadership have you observed/experienced in your lifetime? Describe one of these changes.

3. Referring to the 5 degrees of initiative a leader can exercise (pp. 124-125), what degree do you see exercised most by church leaders right now? Support your answer with at least three examples.

4. What difference do you project in the church of 2001 if church leaders in 1991 practice "strategic leadership" as described in the essay?

5. In your dream for the church of the 21st century, what is your role? How do you picture yourself exercising strategic initiative?

11

Working for God

How much of your life will be spent working?
Most people spend a larger percentage of their lives
at work than at almost any other activity.

Work could be defined as "paid employment," but a
more accurate definition is "activities performed in order to
produce a valuable good or service." When viewed from
this perspective, work includes full- and part-time jobs
performed for pay, household chores, child care, and
volunteer work for churches, service clubs, civic
organizations, and neighbors. Considering various forms of
work leads to the conclusion that a typical North American
probably spends more than 100,000 hours working during
his or her lifetime.

Work is worthy of careful Christian analysis for at
least two reasons. First, work consumes, as already noted, a
great deal of time; a person who wants to understand the

relationship between faith and life cannot afford to neglect the large portion of life devoted to work. Second, a person's work is directly related to his or her sense of identity—ask someone to "tell me about yourself" and you'll likely be given an occupational title. Work guides the formation of various relationships, provides a person with evidence about how well he or she is coping with life, and provides an enduring social role and sense of stability. These dimensions of a person's work are so important that successful experiences at work make a strong positive contribution to spiritual health and emotional well-being.

This chapter is designed to help you understand how work can be related to Christian beliefs. The overall thesis of this chapter is that important truths about work can be seen in the Scriptural account of human origins.

While the Bible focuses on the nature of God and the relationship between God and humanity, it also provides insights into the nature of humanity and the relationship between humanity and the created world. Some of these insights can be developed from the Biblical account of creation. This chapter, using the opening chapters of Genesis as a springboard, will argue that:

1. Though tainted as a consequence of human sin, work remains a blessing from God.
2. The physical world can achieve its full potential only as a result of human work.
3. God has distributed human abilities and interests so that social interaction and commercial activity are encouraged.

Each of these claims will be addressed in a section that follows.

Work as Blessing

The opening chapters of Genesis teach us that God is the Creator and provide some hints about what life would have been like in a sinless world. According to Genesis, God instructed humans to "subdue" and "rule over" (Genesis 1:28) the earth and its creatures. He put mankind in the Garden of Eden "to work it and take care of it" (Genesis 2:15). Work was a part of Paradise.

Perhaps in your experience work has not always seemed like Paradise. That's not surprising—Genesis also describes the unpleasant side of work.

The third chapter of Genesis describes the entry of sin into the world. The first humans chose to disobey God, and their sins resulted in changes in work (and in marriage and parenthood). Adam was told that the created world would no longer be as cooperative as before: "It will produce thorns and thistles" (Genesis 3:18). Consequently work would henceforth include "painful toil" and Adam would live "by the sweat of your brow" (Genesis 3:17-19). So work, a fundamentally good and pleasant activity, became harder and less pleasant. A blessing from God became tainted as a result of human sin.

Many persons have attempted to describe the relationship between humans and work; one very influential description is found in the work of Douglas McGregor. McGregor's work included descriptions of two theories of management, that is, two sets of assumptions that might guide a manager or a company—Theory X and Theory Y. These were not descriptions of specific companies but rather summaries of competing tendencies McGregor had observed in many actual companies. Each theory began with an assumption about the relationship between humans and work. Theory X holds that "the average human being has an inherent dislike of work and will avoid it if he can." In contrast Theory Y holds that "work is as natural as play or rest. The average human being does not inherently dislike work." From a Christian viewpoint Theory Y can be seen as capturing the fundamentally wholesome and natural essence of work, while Theory X reflects the reality of toil in a world tainted by sin.

No one should accept so simple a view as Theory X or Theory Y—experience indicates that humans have mixed feelings about work. For a Christian, these ambivalent feelings confirm the psychological accuracy of Genesis. Humans engaged in productive activities frequently are caught up in "the flow," find time rapidly slipping away, and experience a warm glow of satisfaction. Surely God intended for all work to feel this good. Humans at work also periodically find themselves distracted, weary, and reluctant, or overwhelmed by a stubborn and resistant task. This is a consequence of human sin.

The idea that work is a blessing, albeit a tainted one, has several implications. All managers need to understand the mixed feelings humans have about work, encourage the positive feelings that result from useful accomplishment, and be prepared for the negative feelings that sometimes affect all workers. Human resources (personnel) specialists need the same realistic attitude.

Human resources specialists should remember, in addition, that God intended for humans to "rule over" and "subdue" the created world. This has important implications for job design. The goal of a Christian engaged in job design (deciding what tasks go with which job) and in selection (hiring and assigning persons to jobs) should be to place each person in a job that gives him or her a sense of having a constructive impact on the created world. A Christian knows that machines should serve people not the other way around. Only work that helps a human recognize his or her rightful role as subduer of the earth can be the blessing God intended.

But the benefits of work are not confined to the worker. Benefits also exist for the created world.

A Synergistic System

The work God intended for humans to do was not pointless. Instead, the created world was designed so that human intervention is needed to achieve full potential. The forces of nature and human efforts produce beneficial effects beyond what either could produce alone. The system as God designed it is synergistic, that is, the parts (humanity and the created world) cooperatively working together have a multiplied effect.

At one time no plants grew on the earth because, according to Genesis, two things were lacking, water and cultivation: "No shrub of the field had yet appeared . . . the Lord God had not sent rain on the earth, and there was no man to till the ground" (Genesis 2:5). Then God caused streams (or perhaps a mist—translations differ) to irrigate the ground and created humanity to tend the plants (Genesis 2:6,7).

Observation suggests that God designed the entire creation to flower fully only with the assistance of human activity. The created world has the potential to provide abundant wealth (food, clothing, shelter, and all good things) for human habitation, but this wealth is only a potential in the natural (untended) state and becomes a reality only in response to properly directed human effort. For example, refrigeration has permitted a major improvement in the human diet—fresh dairy products, fruit and vegetables even out of season, unspoiled meat—but the process of refrigeration and the refrigerators used in homes, stores, and trucks are human products. The invention, refinement, manufacture, sales, and distribution of refrigerators are parts of a sophisticated market economy. The consequent improvements in human health and happiness—not to mention the delights of a cold Dr. Pepper or a frozen Snickers bar—result from human management of the world God created.

In previous centuries the population of the earth was much smaller and almost everyone was extremely poor. Humans living in a "natural" state were cold in winter, hot in summer; they ate what they could catch when they could catch it; they harvested fruits, vegetables, and grains when they could find them—grinding the grain with stones (and filling their flour with grit that wore away their teeth). Early humanity was poorly nourished, frequently uncomfortable, and short lived. Only human intervention—beginning apparently with domesticated herds of animals and agriculture—permitted the long slow climb to the current level of population and prosperity. Today we have not only the largest population in the history of the earth but, by any measure, a population that is wealthier than any previous population. We have achieved this because God designed His creation to be a friendly and generous home for humanity.

The human role in deriving wealth from the created world is also glimpsed in remarks Moses made to the Israelites as they entered Canaan. As fulfillment of God's promises the Israelites were entering a period of settled living and increasing wealth (Deuteronomy 8:12-13). They were warned against forgetting God (v. 11) or against thinking themselves responsible for their good fortune (v. 17). "But remember the Lord your God," Moses said, "for it is he who gives you the ability to produce wealth" (Deuteronomy 8:18). Humans can produce wealth only because of God-given talents and because of the way God designed the world. God is the real source of all good things.

Before concluding this section, some attention must be given to the environment. Humans are rightly concerned that human activity can harm the earth while (or instead of) bringing it into full productivity. Christians ought to be concerned about the environment because God intended humans to "tame" the earth, not destroy it.

Environmental fragility is not, however, a reason for hysteria. Throughout history humans have periodically feared they were about to do irreversible damage to the earth, and so far, intelligent human responses have been adequate to correct the problem and provide for greater prosperity. For example, concrete replaced wood for many construction projects—this saved trees and also permitted larger, stronger, safer buildings. Petroleum replaced whale oil for lamps—this saved many whales and also led to the development of gasoline, plastics, and various other useful chemicals. The home God built for humanity has so far proved to be a sturdy one when the residents exercise due care. Christians ought to be concerned about the environment not because they think humanity is alone in the universe but because they know the Landlord.

Encouragement of Commerce
The Genesis account of creation says nothing about trade or commerce. But as soon as additional persons are introduced into the story, they began to specialize their work, focusing on animal husbandry (Genesis 4:2), farming (Genesis 4:2), nomadic herdsmanship (Genesis 4:20), musical performance (Genesis 4:21), and tool manufacturing (Genesis 4:22).

From a human perspective the reason for such specialization is clear—persons differ in their abilities, traits, and interests; consequently, each person is most productive when specializing in a task at which he or she has a comparative advantage (i.e., is relatively more efficient). Furthermore, a society as a whole is most productive when each member of the society is most productive, so specialization increases the total amount of wealth that can be distributed among members of the society. All of this assumes, of course, some mechanism of interchange so that the person who specialized in making bronze tools and wants mutton for supper can arrange to give up one or more tools and to get one or more sheep. Trade and commerce must have come into existence as soon as people began to specialize in their work.

The Bible acknowledges the diversity of economic talents (e.g., Matthew 25:15) but offers little explanation, so the Biblical accounts of spiritual talents may be instructive. The Bible repeatedly affirms that the church contains an assortment of people and that these people differ from each other in spiritual talents and responsibilities (e.g., Romans 12:4-8; I Corinthians 12:14-26; Ephesians 4:11-12; I Peter 4:10). These differences are, the Bible teaches, to require or encourage mutual service, division of labor, and cooperative endeavor. "The eye cannot say to the hand, 'I don't need you!' And the head cannot say to the feet, 'I don't need you!'" (I Corinthians 12:21). Perhaps God has distributed economic talents unevenly for a similar reason, that is, to encourage mutual service, division of labor, and cooperative endeavor. Observation certainly demonstrates that diversities of talent and interest nudge humanity toward commerce and a market economy.

Many first century Christians were members of the merchant class and engaged in various forms of commerce. Lydia dealt in textiles (Acts 16:14). Aquila may have operated a "tentmaking" business and employed the apostle Paul (Acts 18:2,3). These Christians were in frequent contact with their non-Christian neighbors and were encouraged to understand them. Business puts a person in contact with others, so men and women in business tend to have relatively realistic notions of the way the world functions. (A college professor may know what people should eat, but a man or woman managing a restaurant or a grocery store will learn what people actually do eat.)

This means two things. First, it poses a particular challenge for Christians in business. They will have many opportunities to succumb to the values and temptations of the world. Second, it offers an opportunity. Christians in business can help the church to understand the times, the culture, and the people the church would like to reach. Christians in business may face some particular temptations, but they are also a valuable resource for the church.

Conclusion

The ancient Greeks believed in a sharp division between that which was good and spiritual and that which was evil and fleshly. For them the body was an envelope of meat and skin—attractive while young and new, but rapidly deteriorating into a wrinkled, ugly sack—from which the spiritual spark of life longed to escape. As a result they were aghast at the claim that God (a spirit) would take on flesh, and proposed various false explanations (e.g., the theory that Jesus appeared to be a man but wasn't actually made of flesh—I John 4:2,3). They were even more upset by the claim that a body (a piece of dead meat) might be resurrected (Acts 17:31,32). Paul had to remind the Christians in Corinth that Christian doctrine did not look forward to existence as a disembodied spirit but rather existence in a new, changed body (II Corinthians 5:2-4).

Eventually some of the false ideas came together as gnosticism, an especially persistent and destructive heresy that troubled the church for more than a century. Gnosticism carried forward the Greek idea that the physical body with its needs and functions was unspiritual and evil. But the church insisted that the incarnation, God becoming flesh, had really occurred and, consequently, that the body was wholesome.

Today the church is sometimes tempted toward a modern gnosticism. Some Christians long for a spiritual life withdrawn from the masses in the marketplace. The body and its appetites, and the whole process of working to produce and distribute goods and services to meet the needs of humanity may be seen by these Christians as distasteful and unwholesome. Such Christians need to think carefully about the incarnation. They need to remember that God designed the created world to need human work, and distributed talents among men and women in such a way as to encourage commerce.

The Church and the world need men and women who see their work as a blessing from God, as a cooperative effort with God to improve the quality of life for all humanity, and as an opportunity to meet and influence their fellow humans. Are you such a person?

Lamar Reinsch, Ph.D.
Professor of Management Sciences
Abilene Christian University

Works Cited

Beckmann, David M. *Where Faith and Economics Meet: A Christian Critique*. Minneapolis: Augsburg, 1981.

Malherbe, Abraham J. *Social Aspects of Early Christianity*. 2nd ed. Philadelphia: Fortress, 1983.

Maurice, Charles, and Smithson, Charles W. *The Doomsday Myth: 10,000 Years of Economic Crisis*. Stanford: Hoover Institution Press, Stanford University, 1984.

McGregor, Douglas. *The Human Side of Enterprise.* New York: McGraw-Hill, 1960.

Novak, Michael. *The Spirit of Democratic Capitalism.* New York: Touchstone—Simon and Schuster, 1982.

Perlman, Helen Harris. *Persona: Social Role and Personality.* Chicago: University of Chicago Press, 1968.

Worley, David. "Occupations and Preoccupations in Christ." *Institute for Christian Studies Faculty Bulletin* 6(1985): 32-57.

Questions

1. What relationship is there between your faith and environmentalism?

2. Provide your best rationale for Christians caring for the environment. What are you personally doing to care for the environment God has provided for you?

3. What are some of the real challenges/temptations Christians face today in the workplace? What are some temptations you have faced?

4. List characteristics you would look for in work appropriate for Christians? Discuss characteristics you would avoid.

5. Discuss how you can be "in the world" but not "of this world"? How is this a useful distinction?

12

Honor God with Your Body

"Do you know that your body is a temple of the Holy Spirit, who is in you, whom you have received from God? You are not your own; you were bought at a price. Therefore honor God with your body."

(I Corinthians 6:19-20, NIV)

Webster defines temple as a building for the worship of God. The first temple of God, which served as God's dwelling place for 400 years, was the Tabernacle. Solomon's glorious temple became the first permanent structure for God's people when it replaced the Tabernacle in 960 B.C. However, Solomon's temple was destroyed by the Babylonians in 586 B.C. Ezekiel had a vision, in 573 B.C., of a future ideal temple restored.

Synagogues arose during the years of captivity for the Jewish nation. Although they were not temples, they were small buildings which served as places of instruction and worship, scattered throughout the Jewish communities. All larger towns had one or more and were presided over by a board of elders, or rulers. Early Christian meetings were modeled in part after the pattern of synagogues.

After returning from captivity, the Jewish people again desired to build a permanent temple to honor God. In 536 B.C. the construction of Zerubbabel's temple began. Due to opposition of the project, work on the temple stopped in 530 B.C. Ten years later work once again was under way and completion occurred in 516 B.C. Zerubbabel's temple stood for 500 years.

Herod's temple was the temple to which Christ came. It was built by Herod, of marble and gold, and was indeed magnificent beyond imagination. Work on Herod's temple had begun in 20 B.C. and was not finally completed until A.D. 64. It was destroyed by the Romans six years later.

Temples were holy places regulated by strict God-given laws. Failure to follow some of these laws, such as entering the most Holy places, could result in instant death. Temples served as centers for God to draw His people close to Him. They represented the focal points of life. However, make note that these earthly temples were built with God's permission and later destroyed by the hands of man.

The New Temple

Temple in the New Testament is considerably different, yet, just as in the Old Testament, it is a dwelling place for God. Although church buildings are sometimes called temples of God, there is no such designation in the New Testament. Jesus tells us in John 4:20-24 that earthly temples were not necessary to the worship of God.

Jesus referred to his body as a temple in John 2:19-20. Collectively, the Church is called a temple of God (I Corinthians 3:16-19). God's dwelling place in the world is established when His Church assembles. Each individual Christian is a temple of God. Our bodies are temples because the Holy Spirit, given by God, lives in each of us (I Corinthians 6:19). Could it be that our bodies are of the same grandeur as Solomon's temple?

The ultimate temple will be in heaven (Hebrews 9:11). Man-made temples are only copies of the true temple built by God. The sacrifice Jesus made allows man's fleshly temple to enter this heavenly temple and live in God's sanctuary for eternity. Just as temples of old, our fleshly temples come into existence with God's permission. Most of the time fleshly temples are destroyed prematurely by man's own hands through neglect, improper lifestyles, and other self-destructive behaviors.

Temples Abused

Jeff, a high school senior, felt he was ready for the adult world. After all, he was 18 years old and could vote and enlist in the armed services. This instant freedom gave him all the privileges of adulthood, so he thought. If he wanted to experience sexual activities—why not? He was an adult. The best way to find out if you want to be married to someone is to sleep with that person first. Besides, knowing if compatibility exists will lessen the chances of divorce. Experience will make for a better husband when marriage does occur. Everyone is doing it, he told himself. All of these arguments and others ran through Jeff's mind as he convinced himself to engage in sexual activities which were in direct opposition to God's laws.

What Jeff did not realize was that he was using God's temple in a most disgracing manner. Ephesians 5:3 says we are to avoid even a hint of sexual immorality, because these are improper for God's holy people (holy temple). Because Jeff did not follow the laws established by God, he now has AIDS. Sexual abuse of his body is now destroying the glorious temple of God.

Janice is enjoying her sophomore year at college. Physical fitness seldom is a concern since she is young and can do most anything she desires. Middle-aged people need to work on physical fitness and she will consider it when she reaches that age. She is also convinced that the carry-over value of athletics during her senior year in high school has kept her physically fit.

Yet, she can not walk three flights of stairs without becoming out of breath. Due to her limited fitness level and over-weight condition, her playing time in intramural basketball is limited to a couple of minutes at a time.

Janice has developed a lifestyle which excludes maintaining a fit temple. Developing fitness requires self-discipline, which Janice does not possess. She has failed to realize that her body needs to be exercised regularly and provided with a healthy diet in order to function properly. An unfit body is destined for physical problems and a premature death. Her temple abuse will become more noticeable as the years go by.

Scott considered himself a good Christian. Since alcohol was readily available, as a high school student he was tempted like everyone else. He was convinced that it was okay to drink. After all, everyone else drank. Even Bible class teachers had admitted it was only a sin if you get drunk. Consequently, during his sophomore year he began drinking.

Control was easy at first. But, as he went places he should not and associated with those of like nature, things began to change. Even though he knew his parents would not approve, he also knew he could quit any time he wanted.

Now he finds himself in college and his drinking habits have not changed. He has been drunk many times, but still believes he can stop drinking anytime he wants. New-found freedom to do the things he wants has not been good to Scott. His lifestyle has become dangerous to himself and others because of his driving under the influence.

Scott does not understand why his friends and parents are concerned. After all, alcohol is legal and his parents have been known to drink a little wine or a beer every now and then. So what if he drinks a little too much on occasion? It's his body and his life and he has a right to do what he wishes.

The truth is, his body is not his own. It is the temple which God has given Scott to use. Jesus died for his temple. Alcohol is a drug which can lead to addiction, even though it is legal. It is also harmful to the body in as small amounts as one or two beers. Alcohol abuses the temple in any amount because it changes normal body functions.

Sharon has an eating disorder. She would be diagnosed as being bulimic, if examined by a physician. Secrecy has been her lifestyle. However, it has become more difficult for her to hide the problem. She always sees herself as being fat. Why does she eat a meal and then cause herself to vomit? Although she does not understand the reasons, she desires be get rid of this curse.

Eating disorders usually develop as a result of events which occur earlier in life. Counseling will be necessary for Sharon to conquer her disease. In the meantime, her body is suffering great harm and her health is at high risk. If only she knew there is help and a cure for eating disorders.

Several theories exist as to how or why bulimia develops. It could be a response to psychological stress. Another theory suggests that bulimia is a manifestation of the drive to become the "ideal woman," which in our society has come to mean slim and trim. Bulimics tend to have low self-esteem and a weak sense of identity which begin early in life. Some research indicates that as many as 20 percent of females on some college campuses are bulimic. However, the point of concern is that Sharon is abusing her body (God's temple) and help is needed.

Uplifted Temples

Bill has been obese for as long as he can remember. For years he has wished he could lose weight and be slender. His efforts have always resulted in failure.

Bill's life has changed recently. Finally, he has found the strength to accomplish his life-long dream. He now realizes there is truth in the statement found in Mark 10:27, "all things are possible with God." With the faith that God was on his side, Bill was able to reach new heights. Now he really believes he can be healthy and maintain a normal body weight.

His new-found strength helps him to view his body as a special gift from God. His desire to please and serve God encourages him as he honors God through maintaining a healthy body. Bill has conquered his weight problem and is successfully working on other weaknesses in his life.

Susan has always struggled with relationships. Even in the elementary grades she had difficulty maintaining extended friendships. She did not know why, but she always seemed to become angry with her friends and arguments resulted. She was never in the wrong and everyone was out to get her. There were times when she would become so angry that she would become physically sick. Her body suffered because anger was an emotional problem which she could not control.

Study of God's word and a lot of prayer have helped Susan deal with her anger. She still becomes angry at times, but now she knows how to deal with it. Anger and hot temper are causes of many sins. Stirring up anger produces strife (Proverbs 29:22; 30:33). Susan now believes these teachings and they have made a difference in her life. She also is guided by Ephesians 4:26, "In your anger do not sin: Do not let the sun go down while you are still angry and do not give the devil a foothold." James 1:19-21 tells Susan to be slow to become angry because man's anger does not bring about the righteous life God desires.

Now that Susan has allowed God to guide her life and is controlling her anger, she feels better. Her body is no longer stricken by stress or sickened from anger. Life is more enjoyable and she is able to accomplish so much more for God, for others, and for herself. Relationships have become positive influences in her life and her temple is an example for others.

Ways To Honor God With Your Body
1. Keep your body in a fine-tuned physical condition.
2. Avoid using drugs that harm the body.
3. Provide it with a nutritionally sound diet.
4. Allow it the proper amount of sleep and rest.
5. Use your body as a positive example for others to follow.
6. Keep your body from sexual immorality.
7. React to stress in a positive and healthy manner.
8. Maintain a high standard of cleanliness.
9. Use prescription and over-the-counter drugs wisely.
10. Be wise by developing a disease-prevention lifestyle.

Dickie Hill, Ph.D.
Professor of Health, Physical Education and Recreation
Abilene Christian University

Questions

1. In the examples of Jeff, Janice, Scott, and Sharon, what general rationale led to harming their bodies? What resulted from rationalizing and giving in?

2. How is proper care of the body a matter of faith? In other words, explain the link between care of the body and faith.

3. Name one area of care for the body in which you see yourself as a good example. Explain how that affects your life positively and how faith helps you maintain that care.

4. Name one area in which you are ineffective or less than effective in caring for your body. Describe how it affects your lifestyle negatively.

5. Where in the scriptures can you draw help for becoming more effective in honoring your body? Where on campus? Who on campus is a good model of the area in which you are ineffective or less than effective?